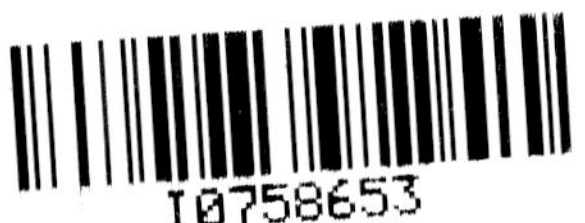

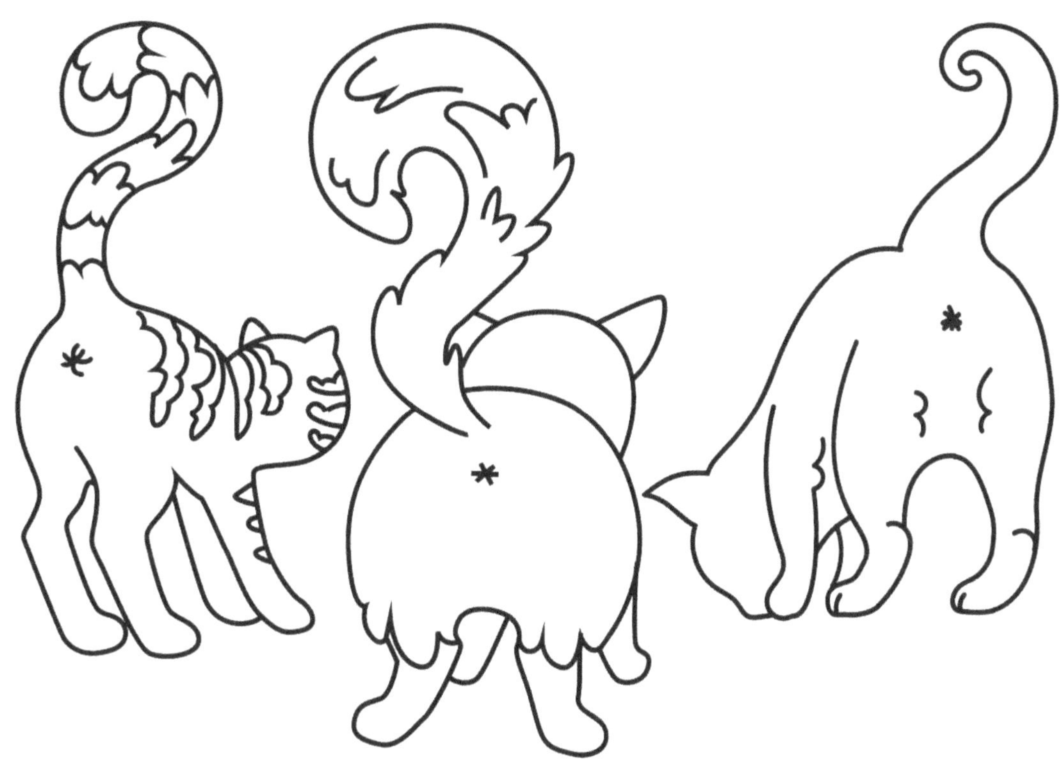

THIS BOOK BELINGS TO

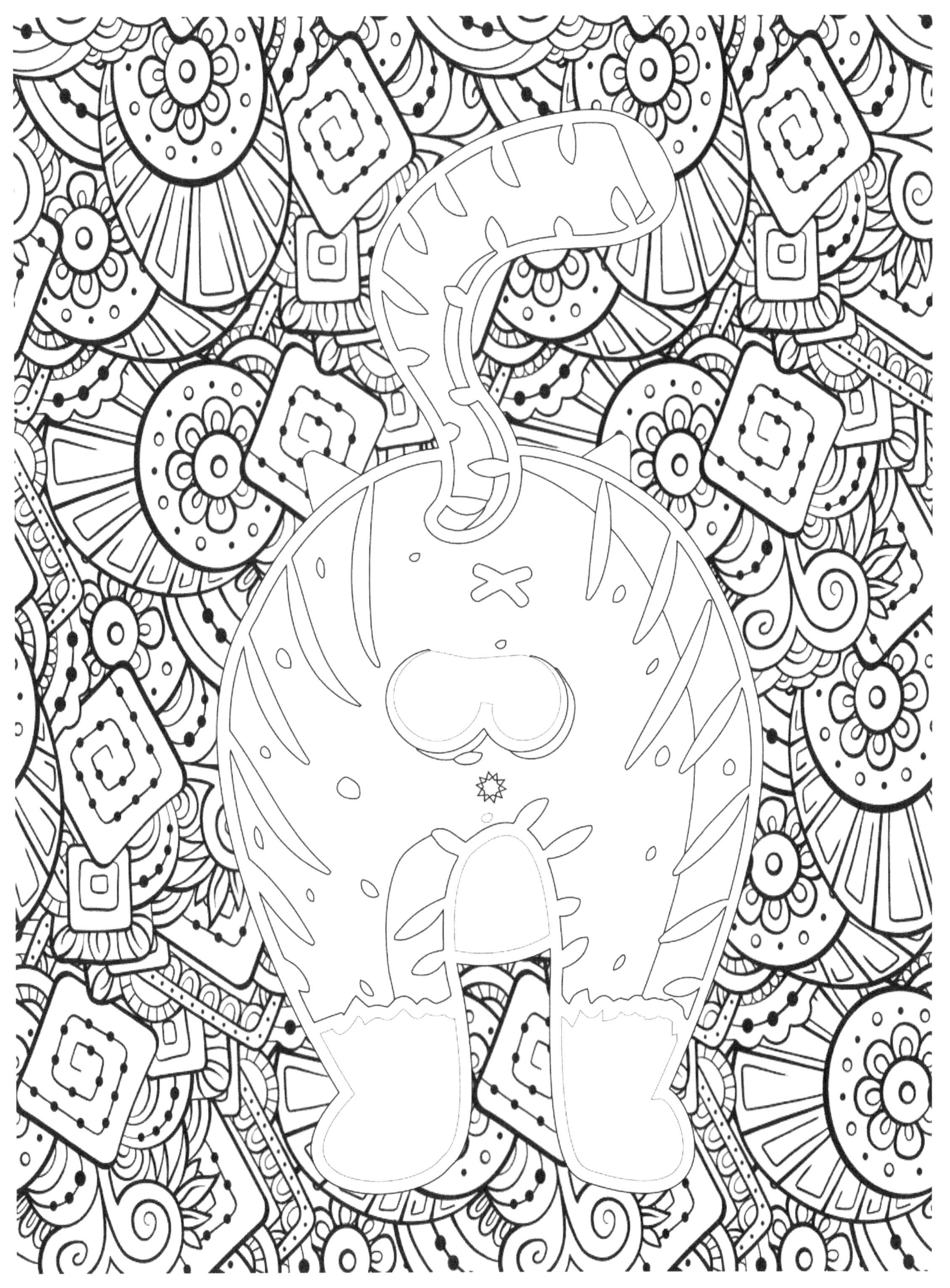

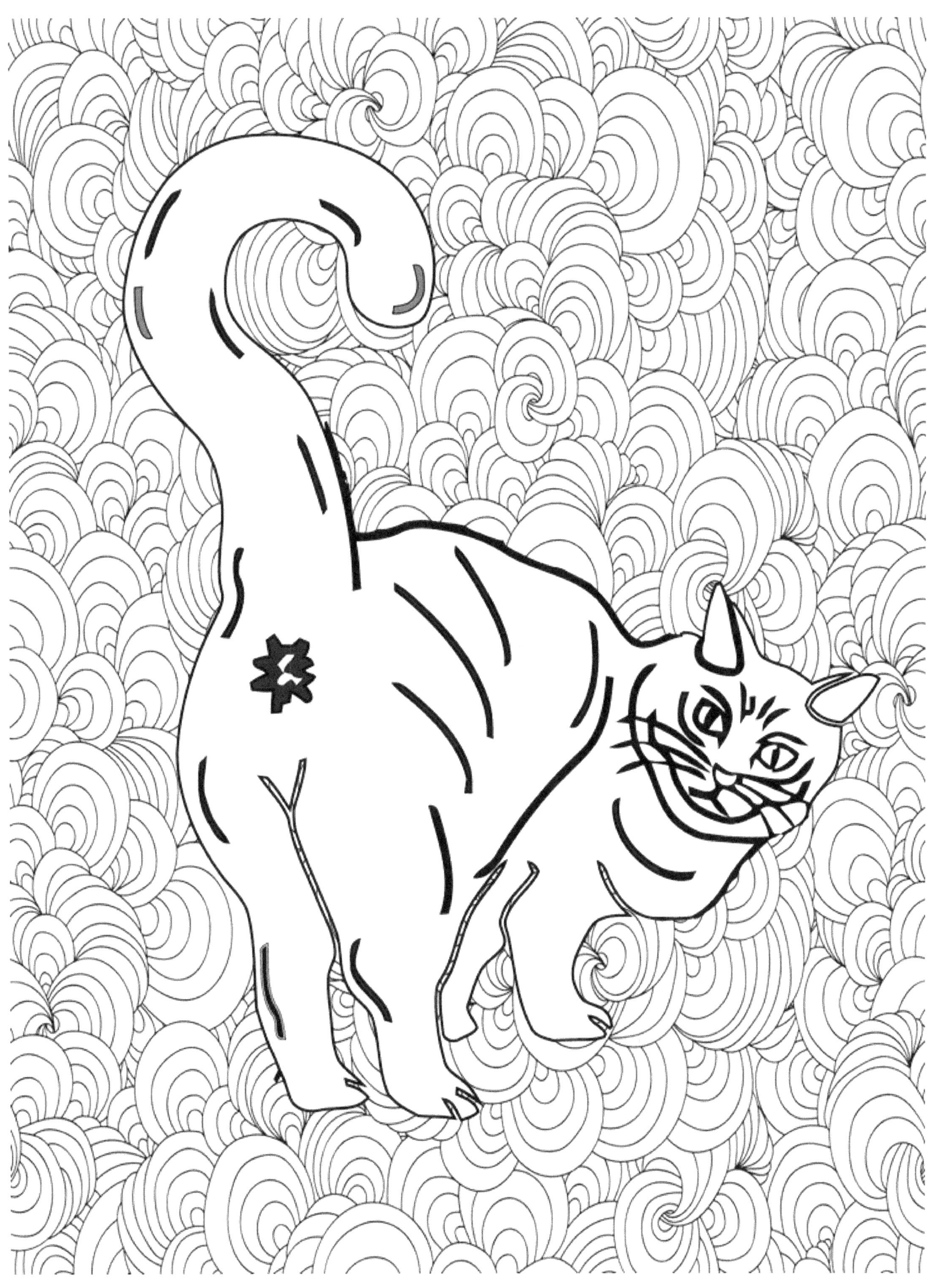

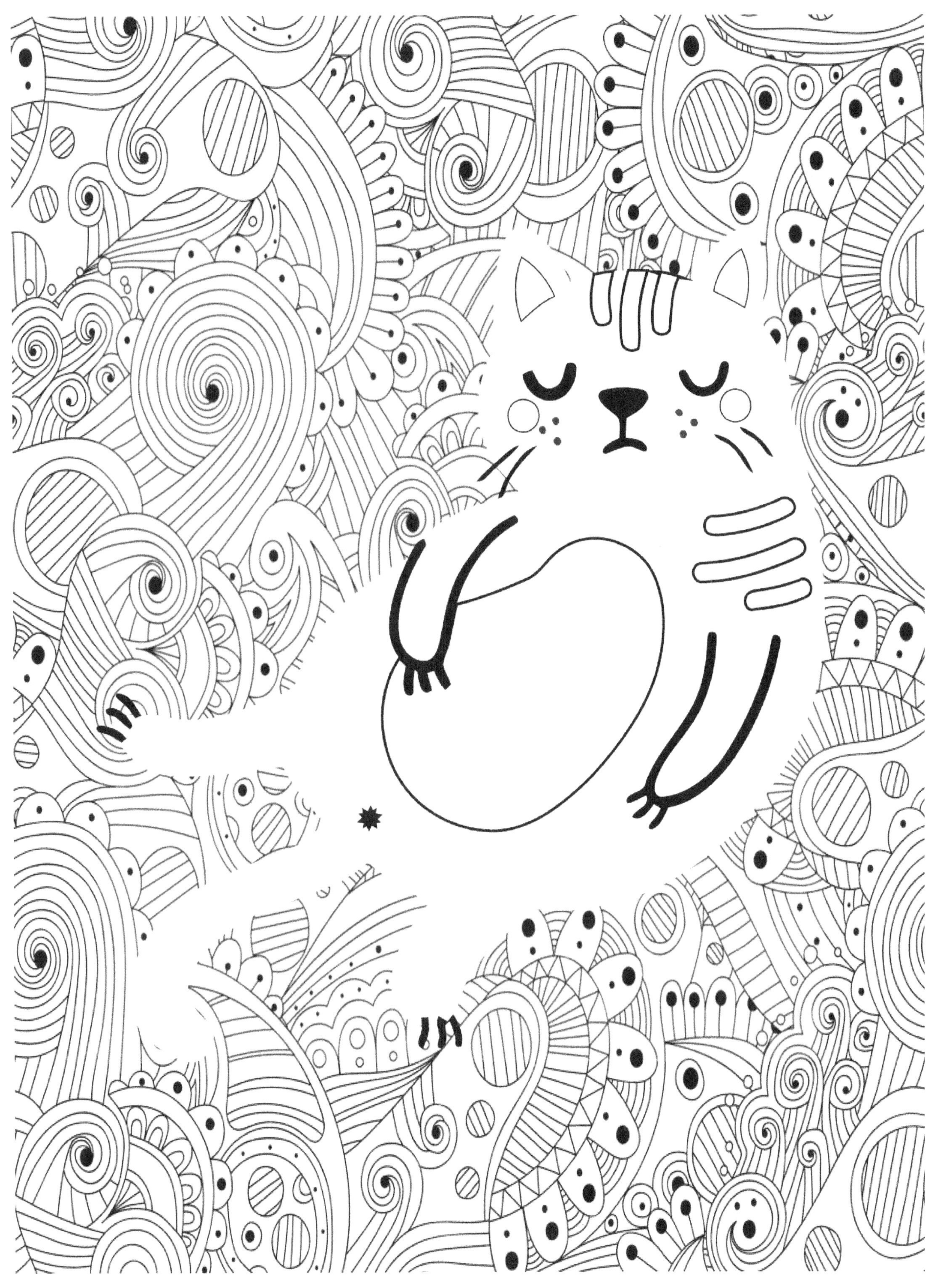

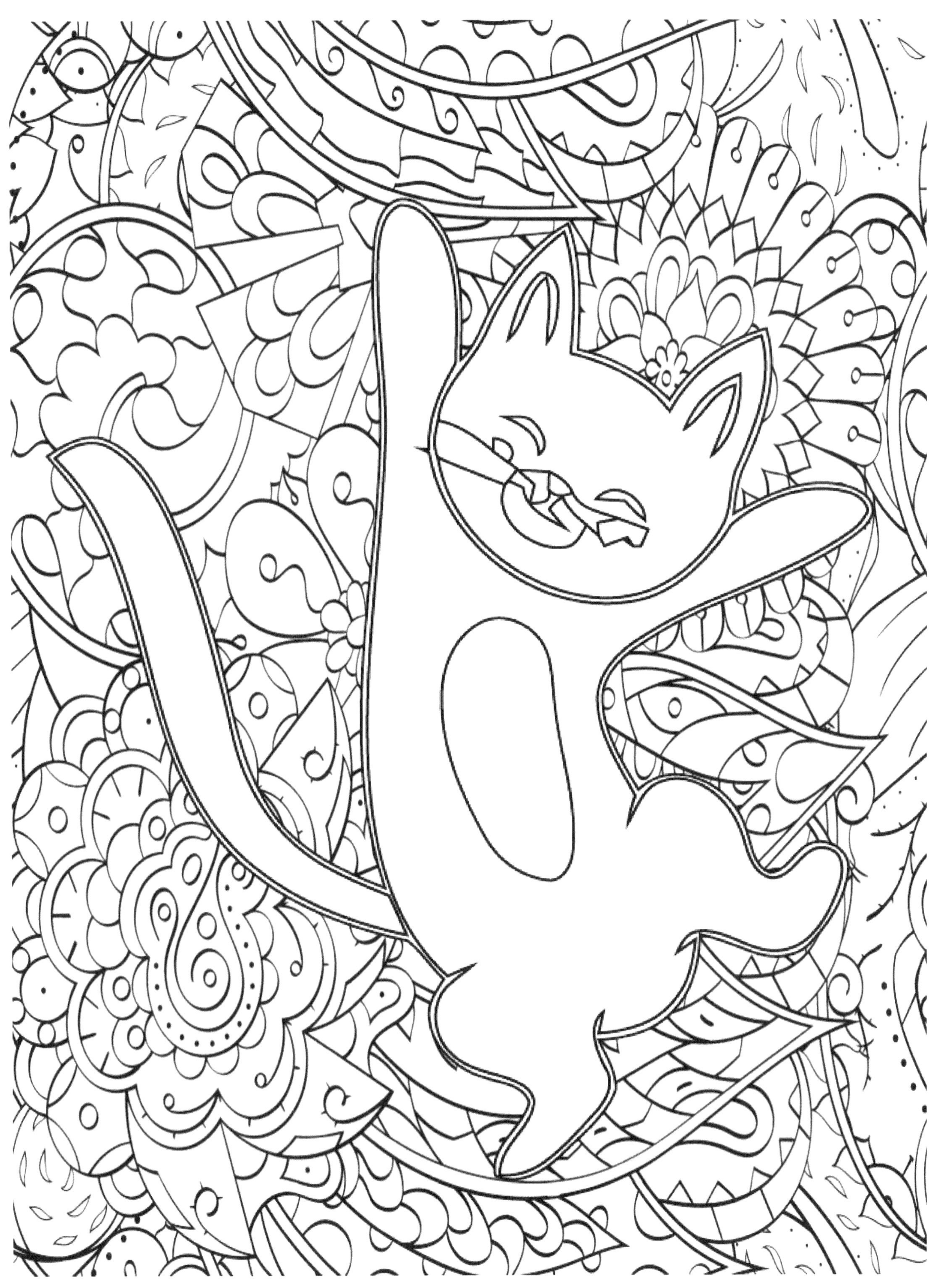

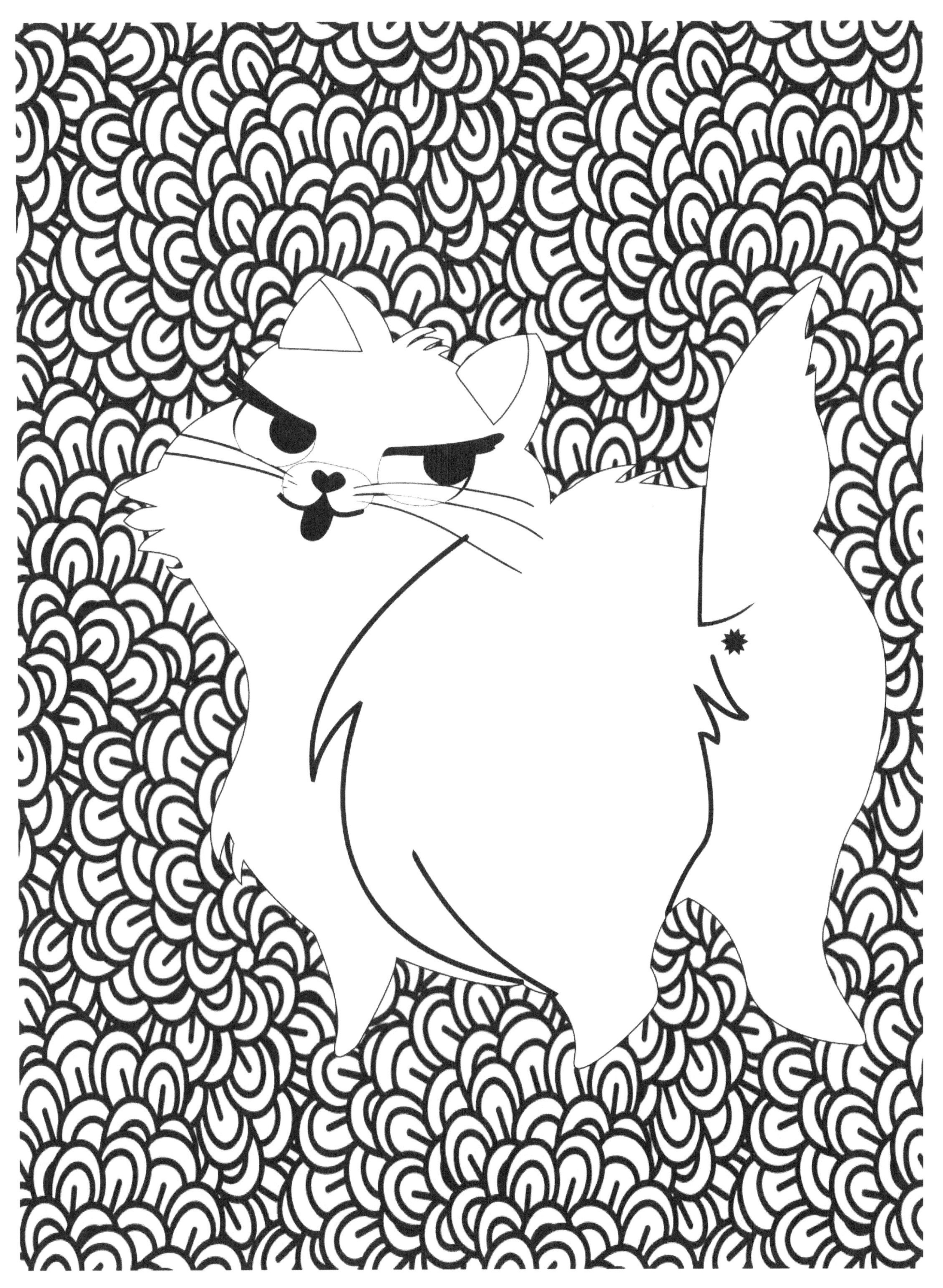

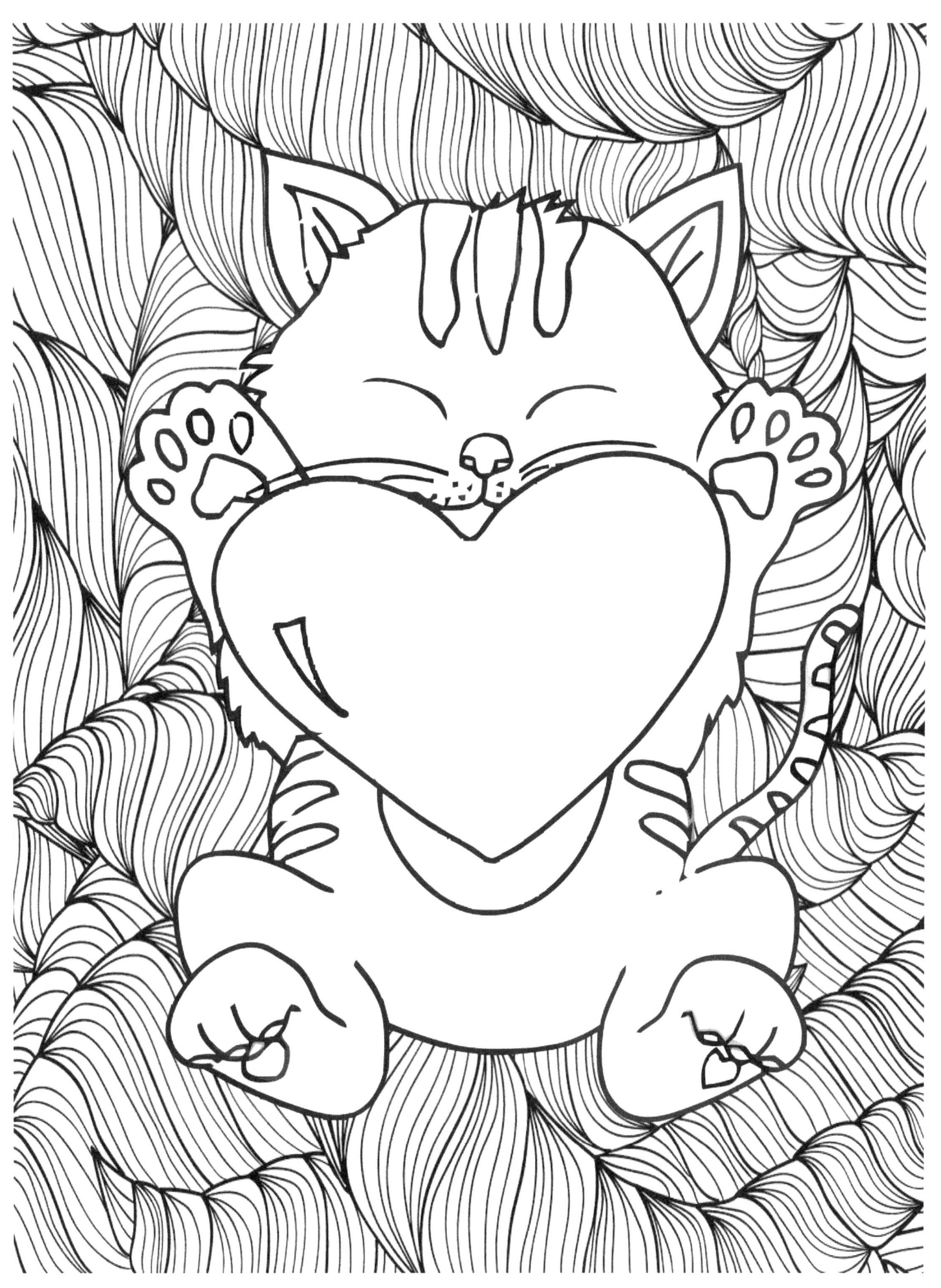

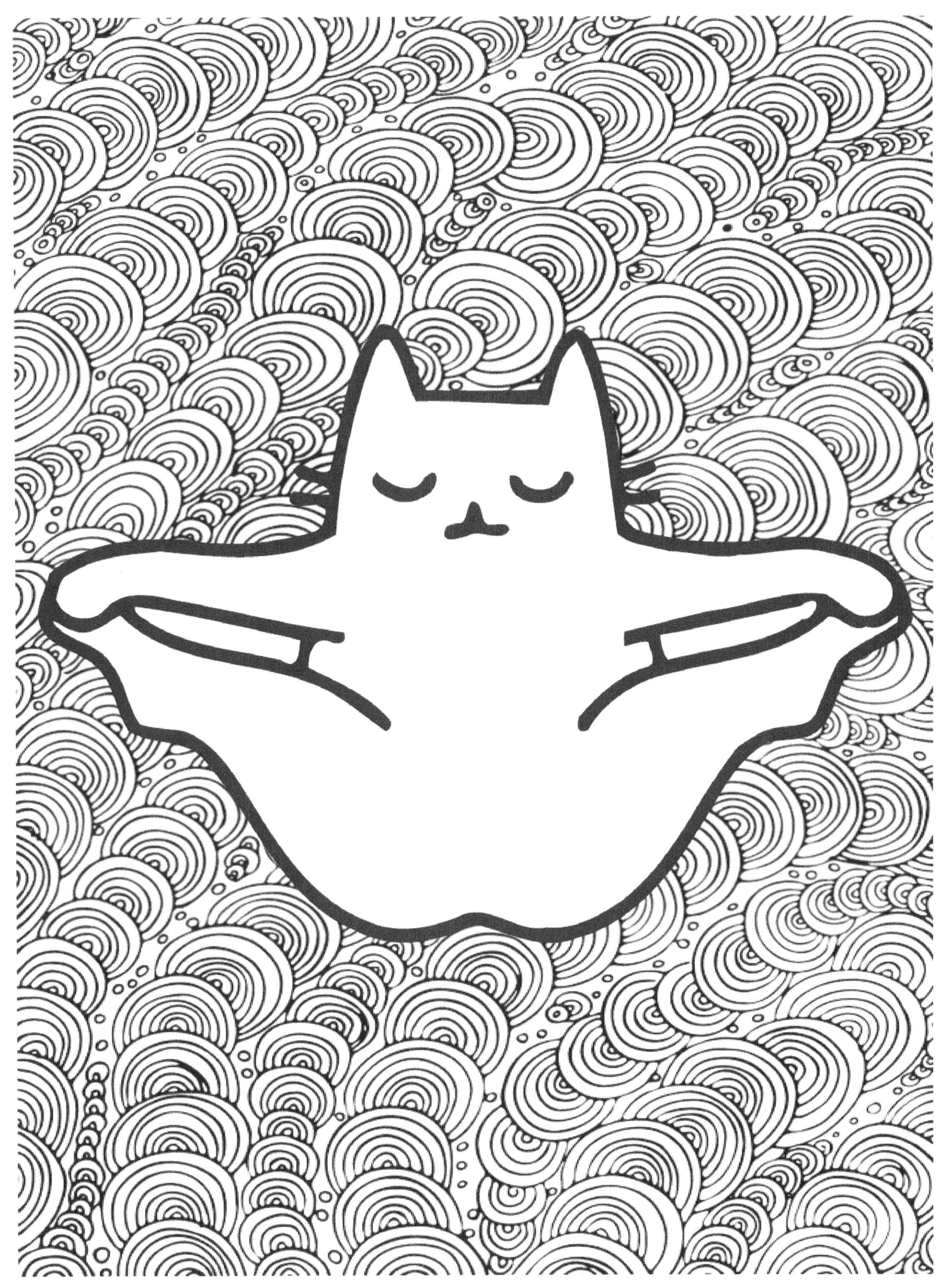

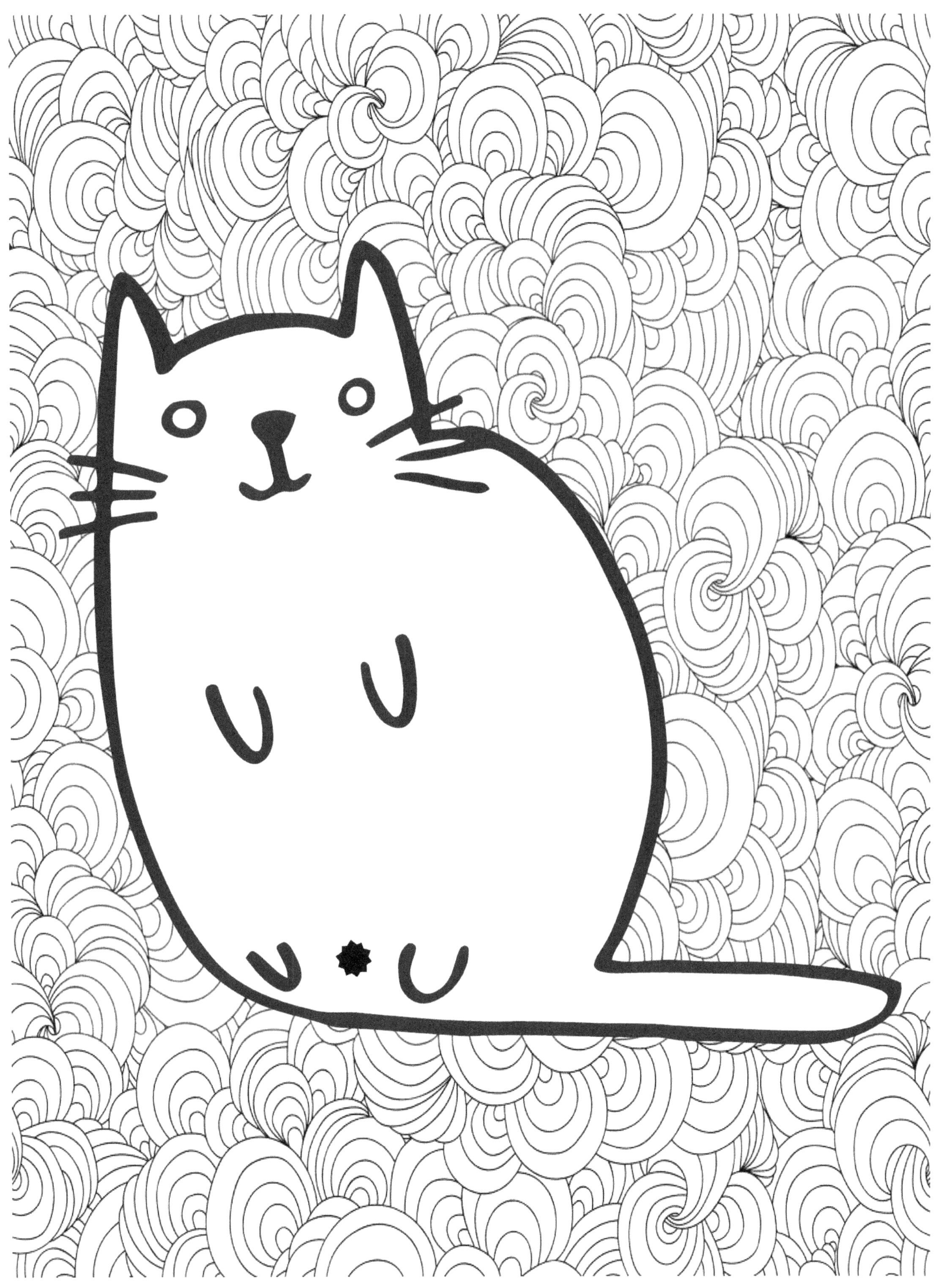

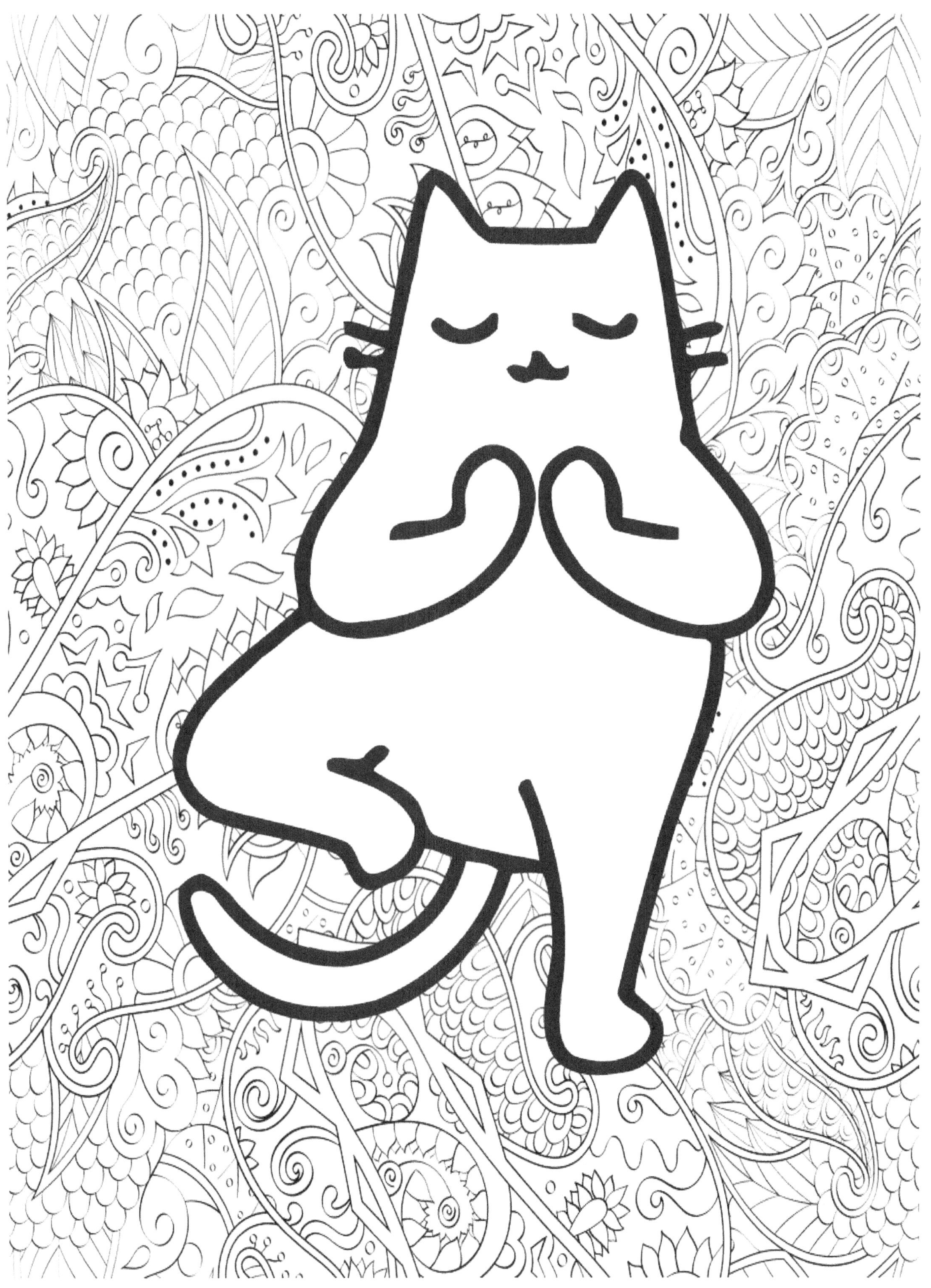

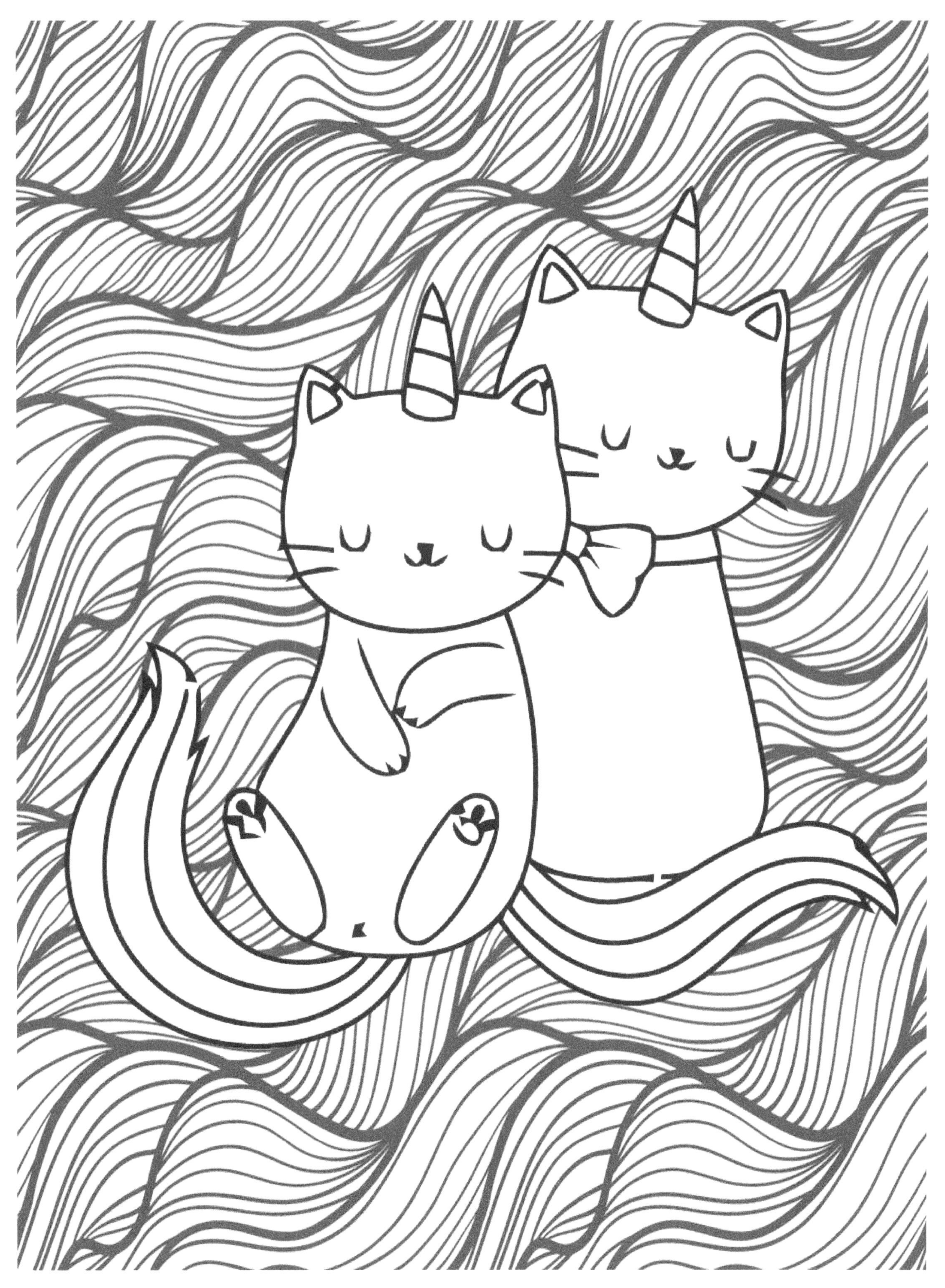

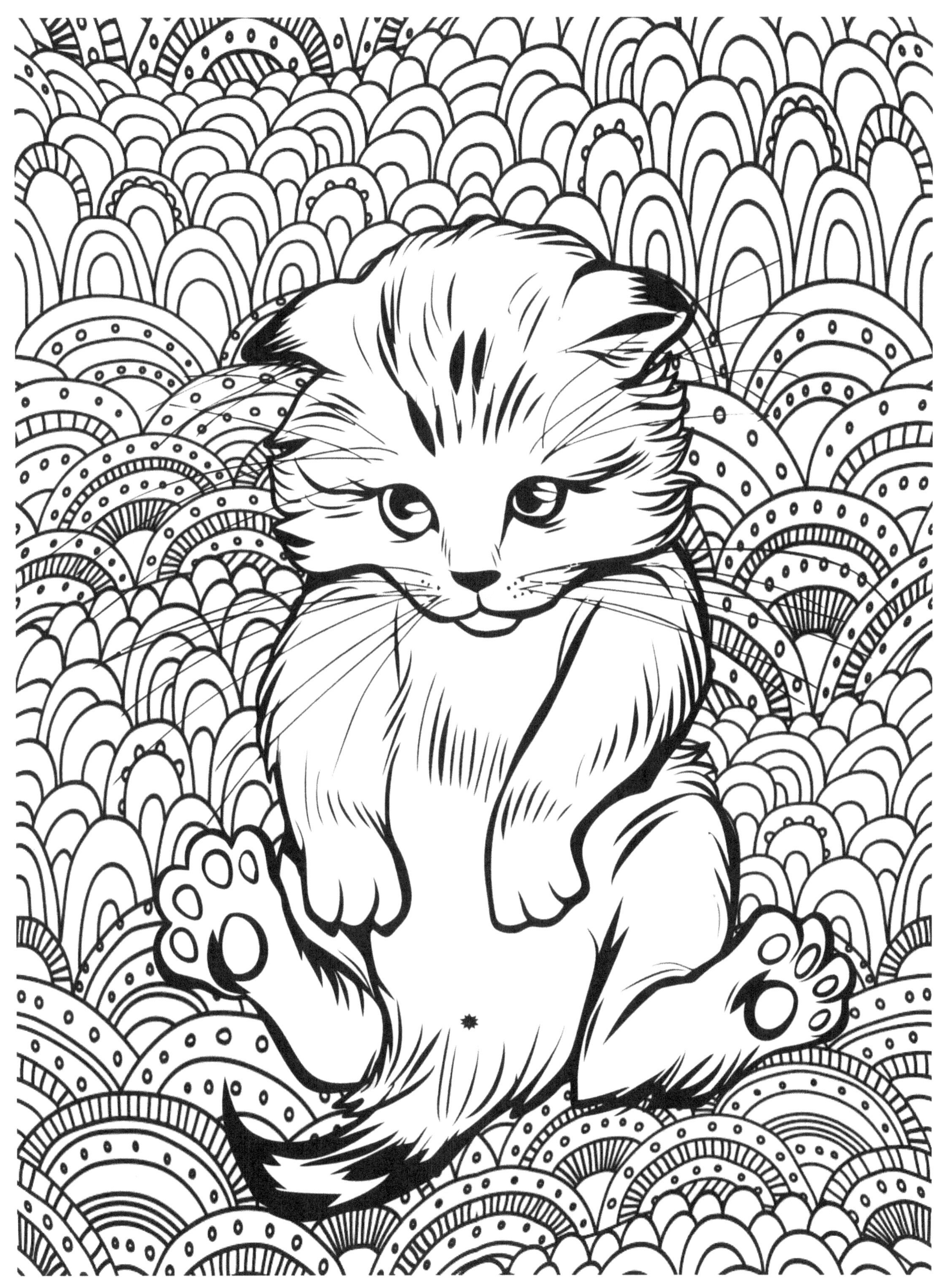

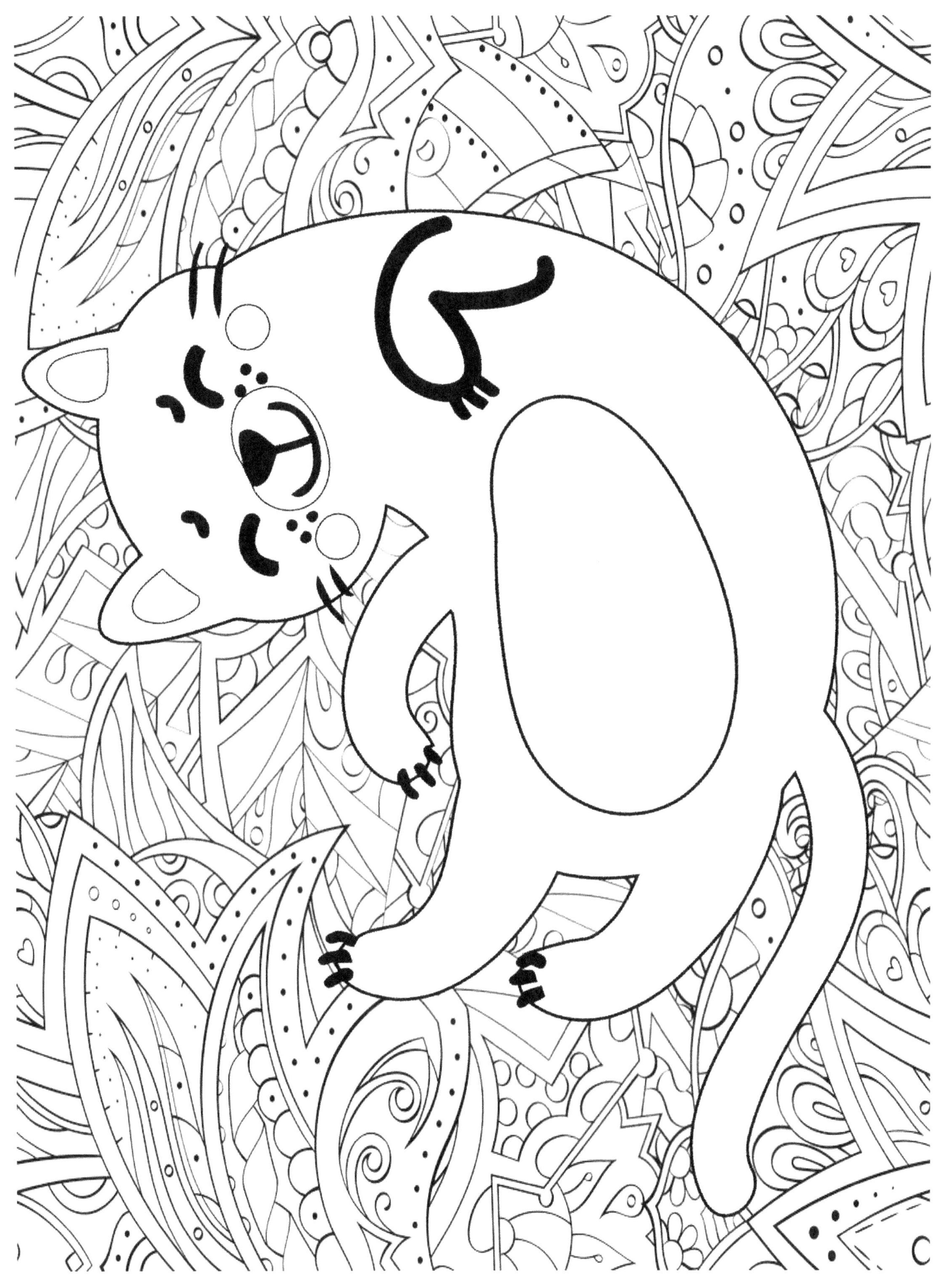

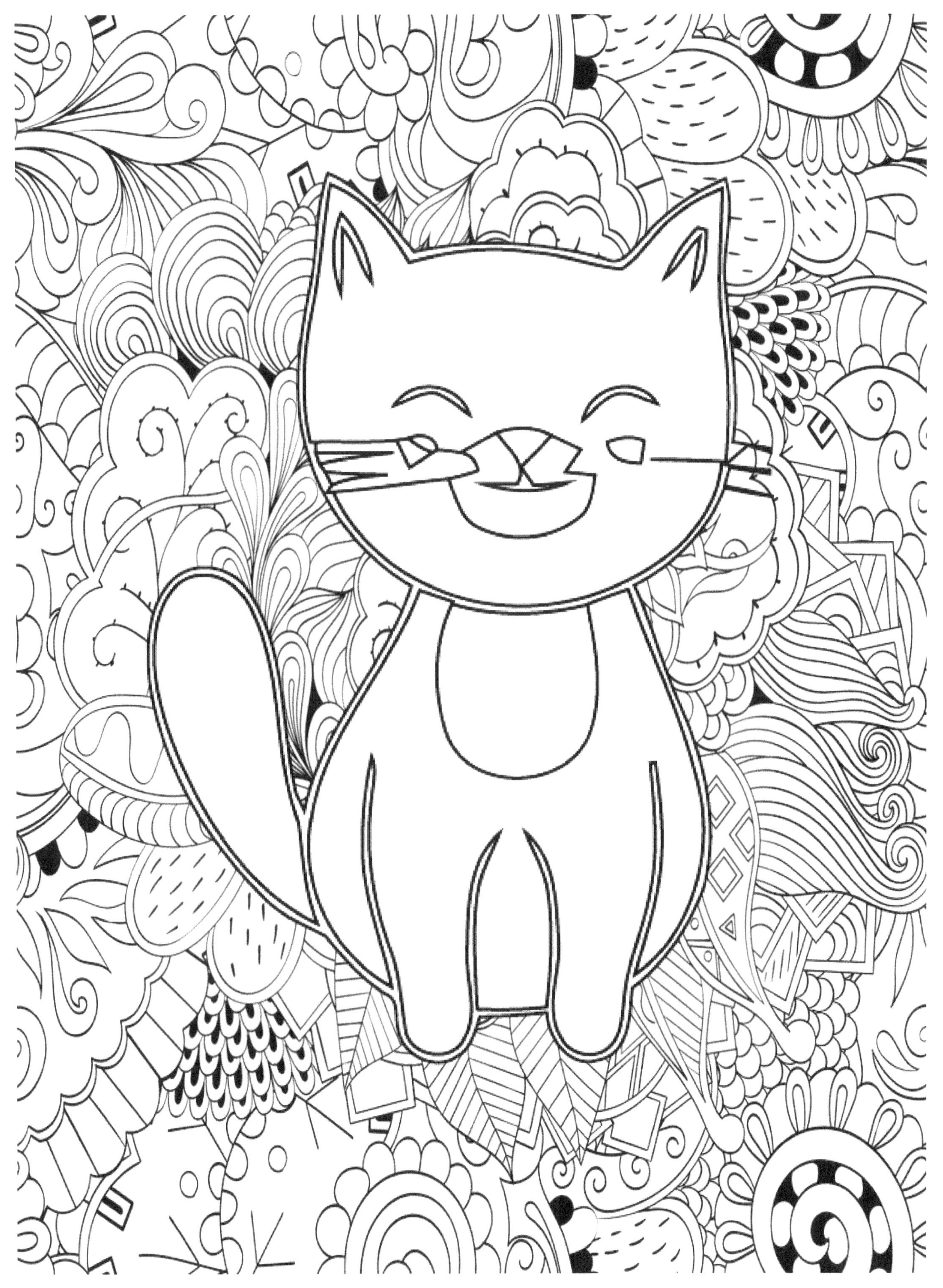

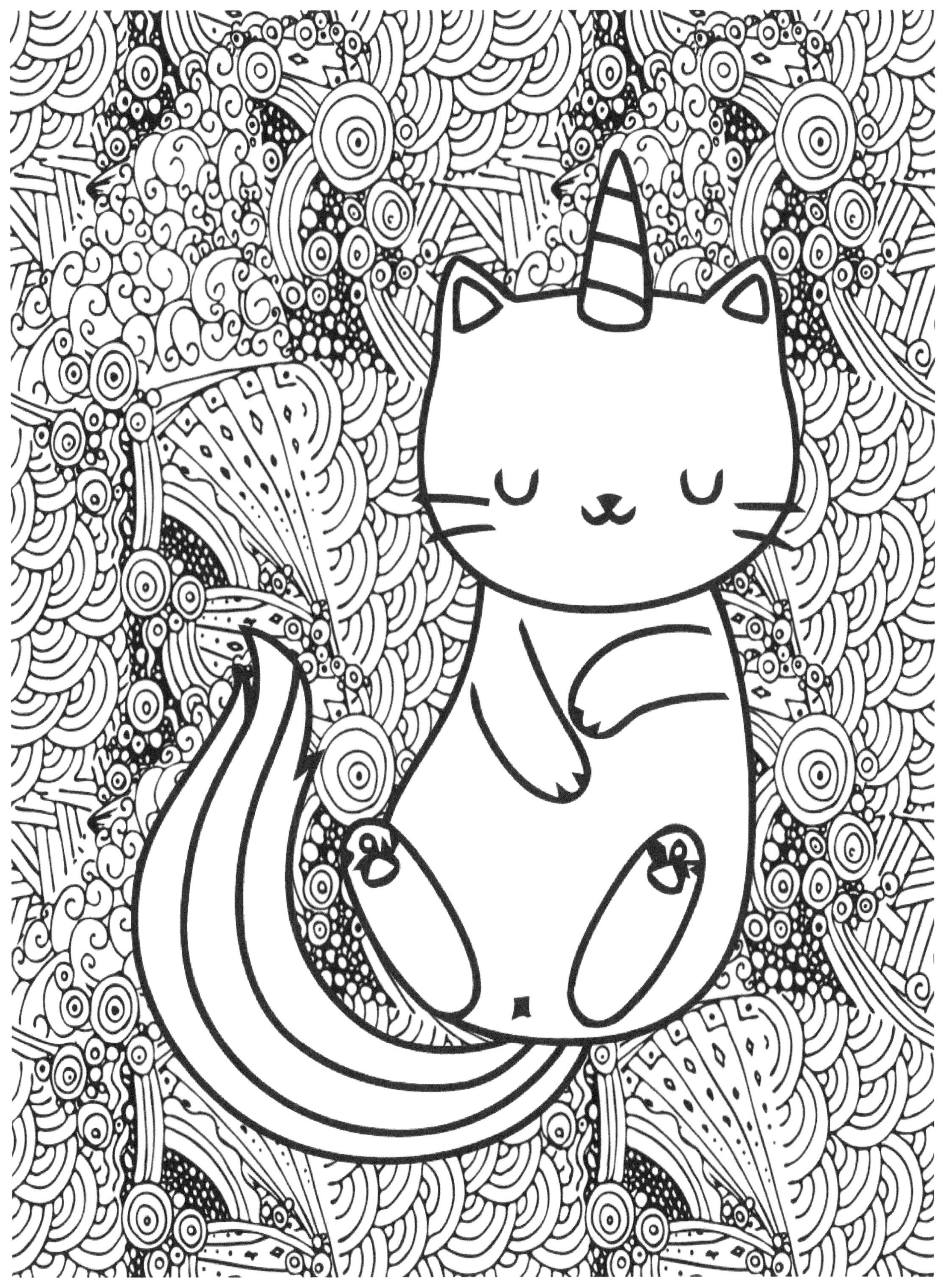

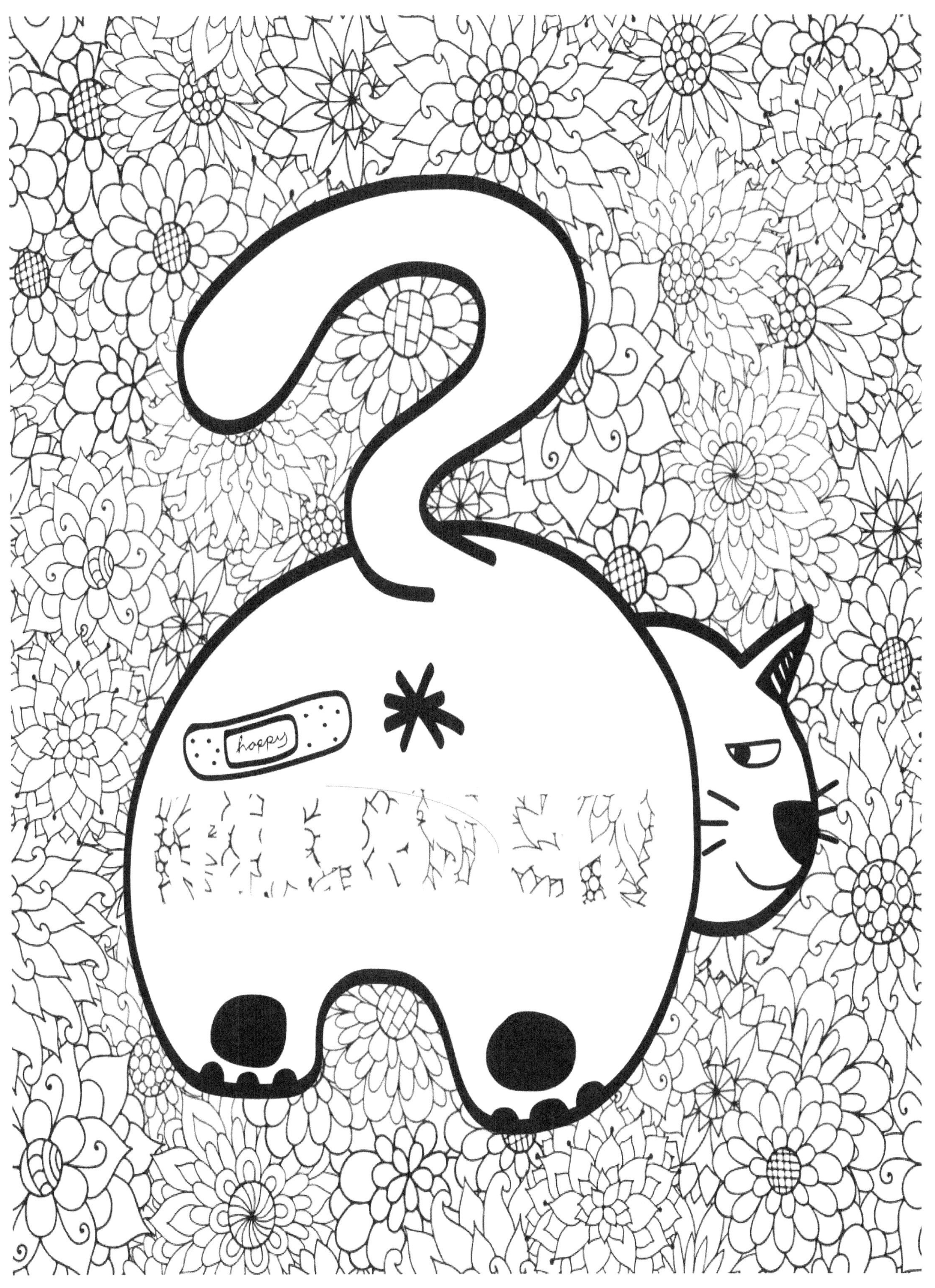
happy

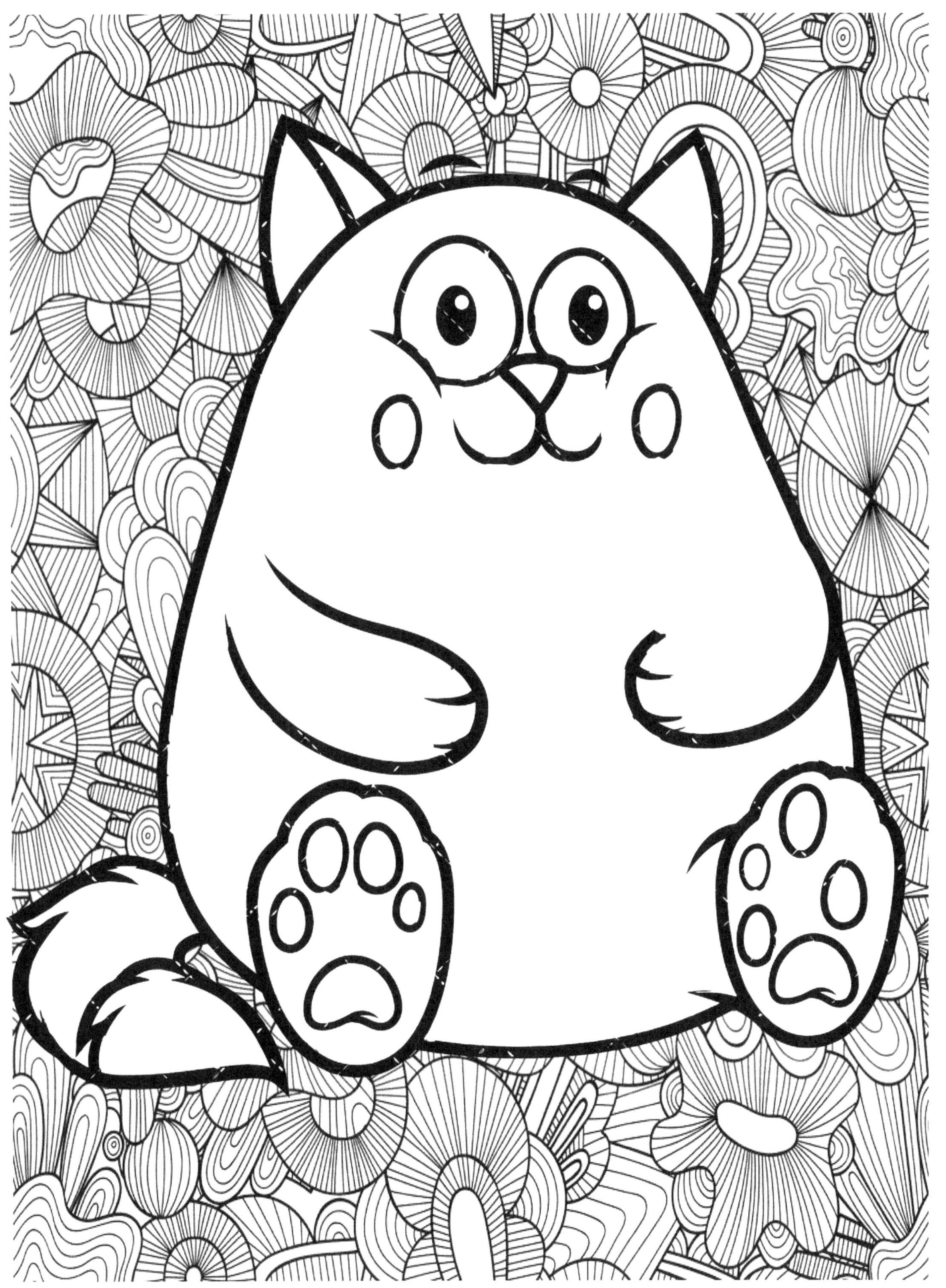

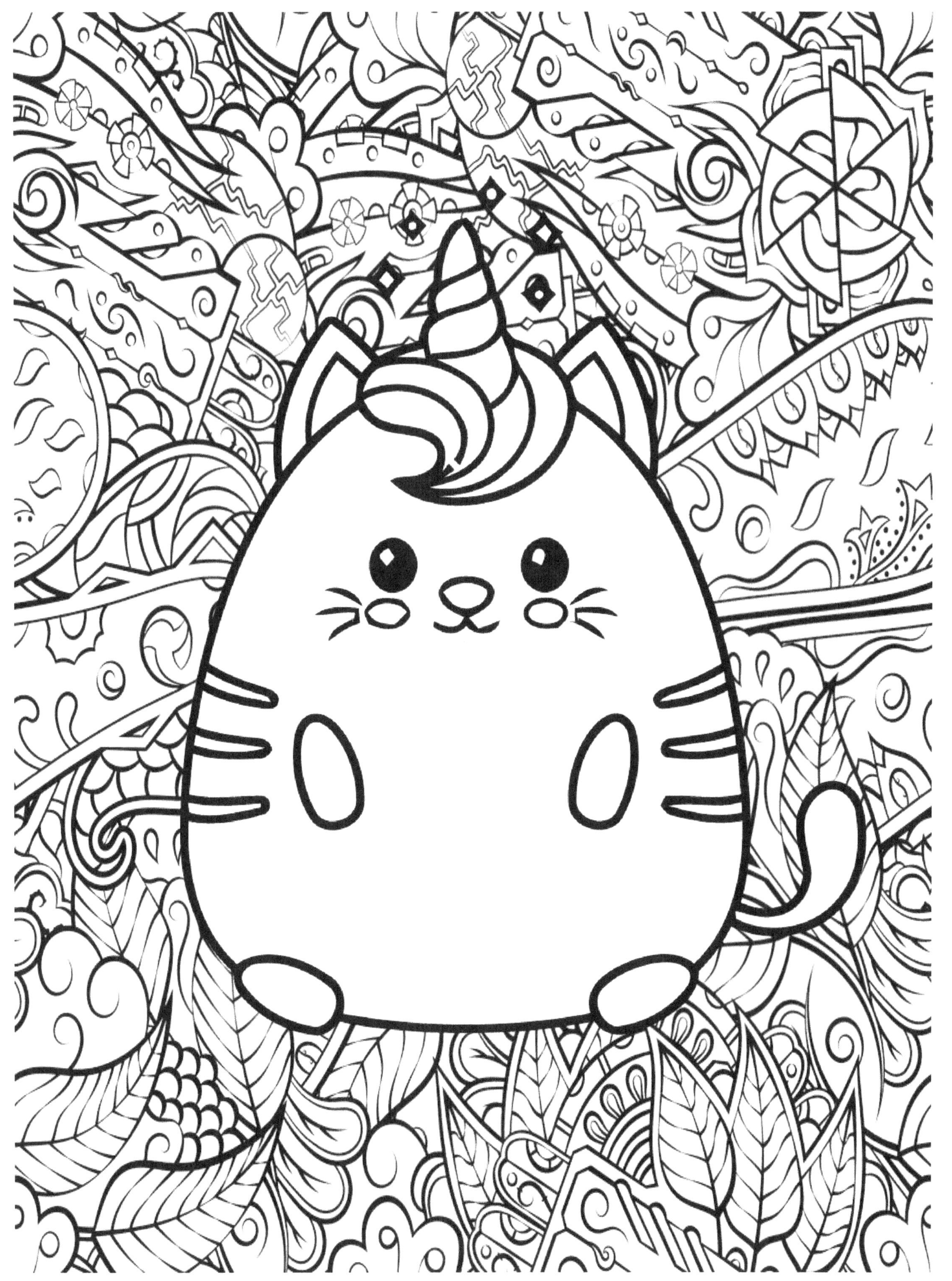

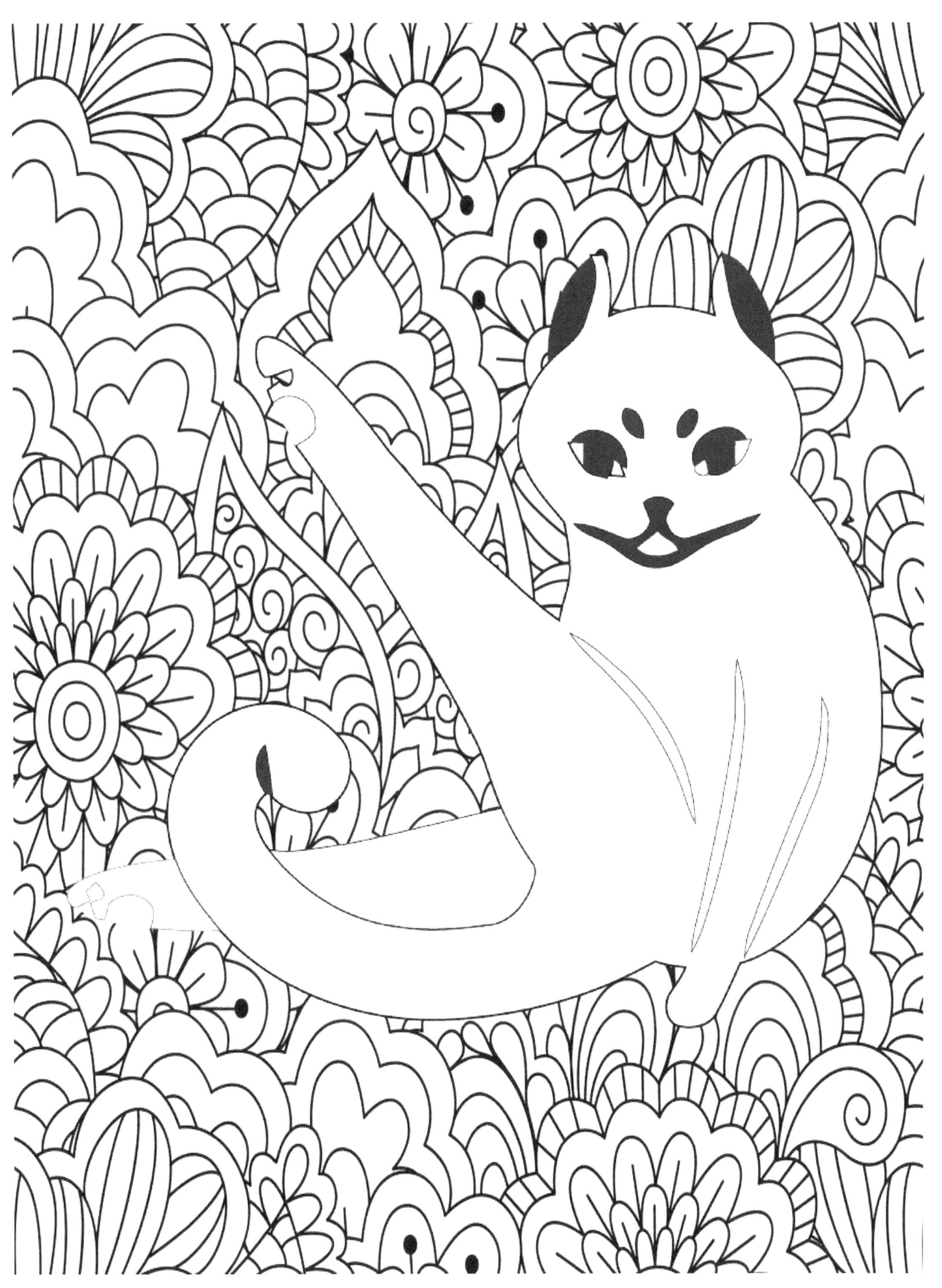

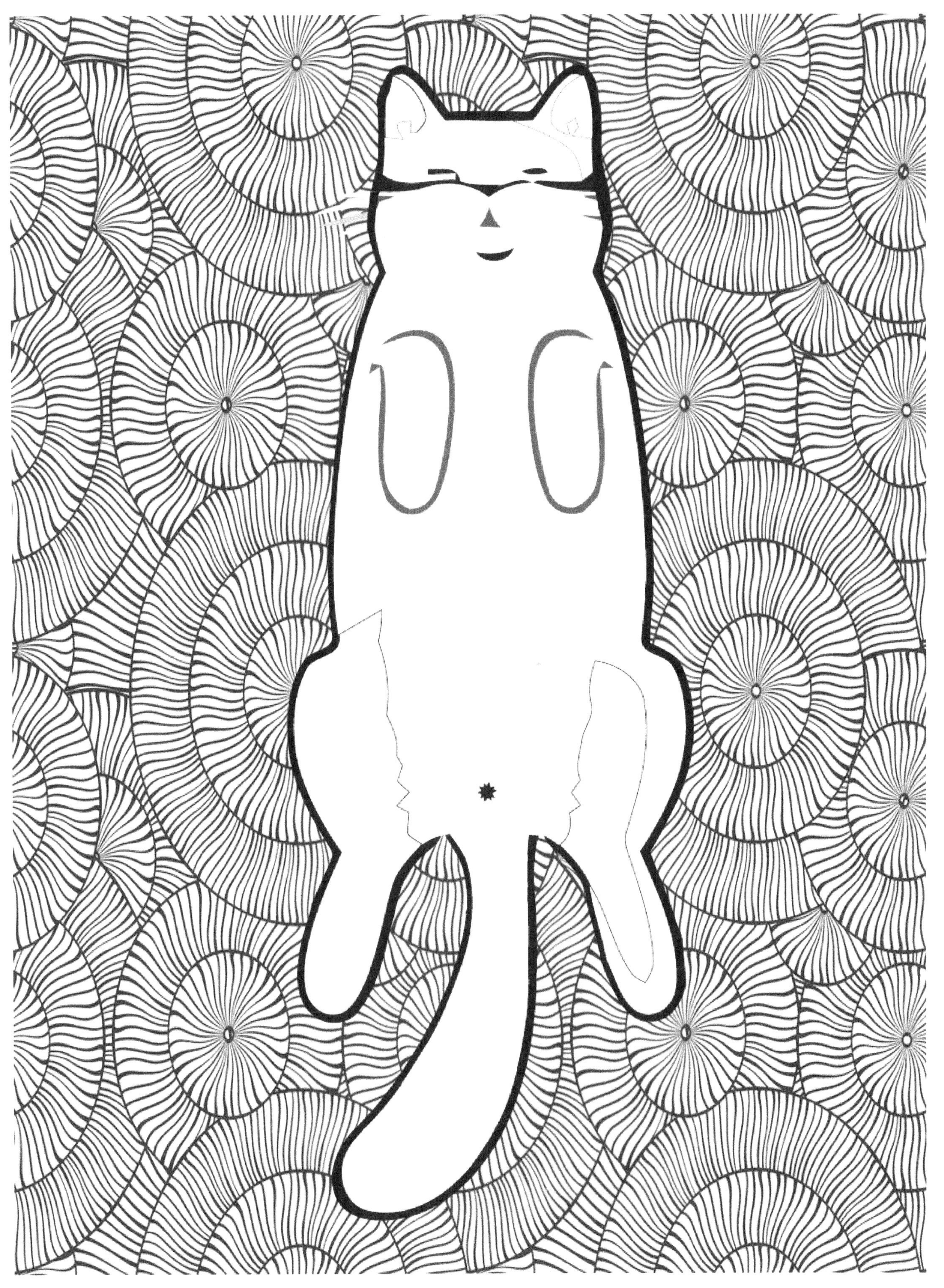

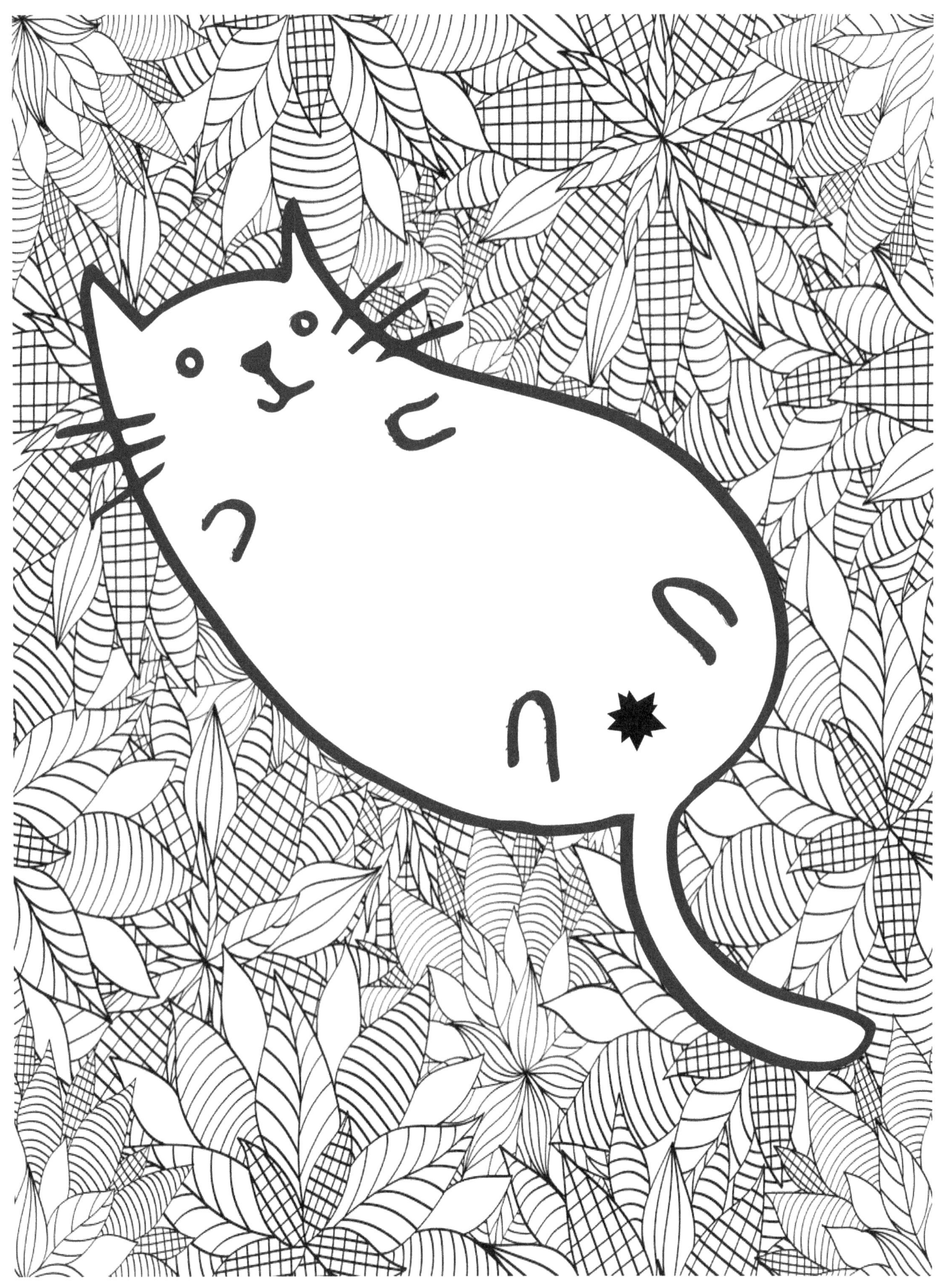

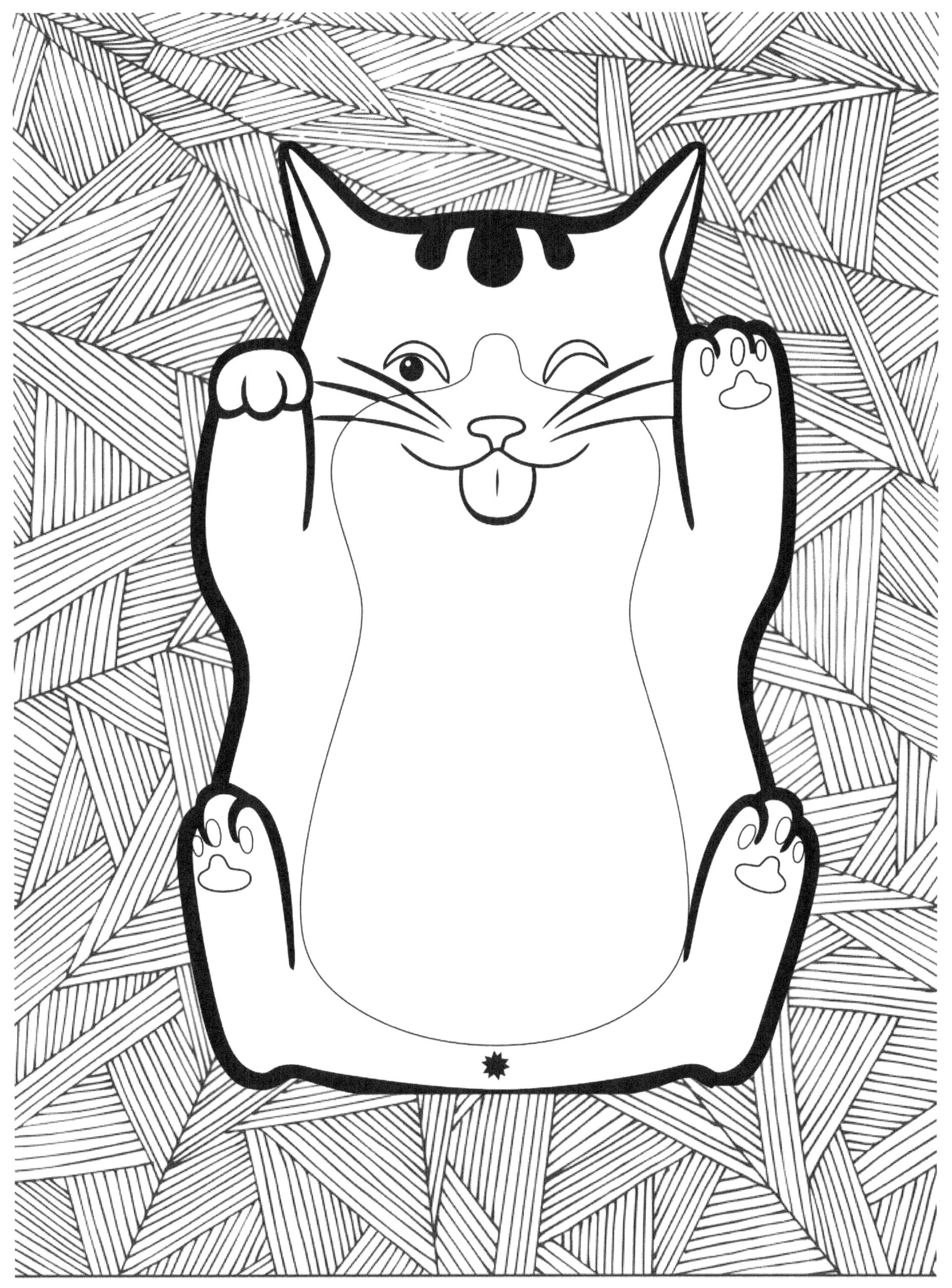

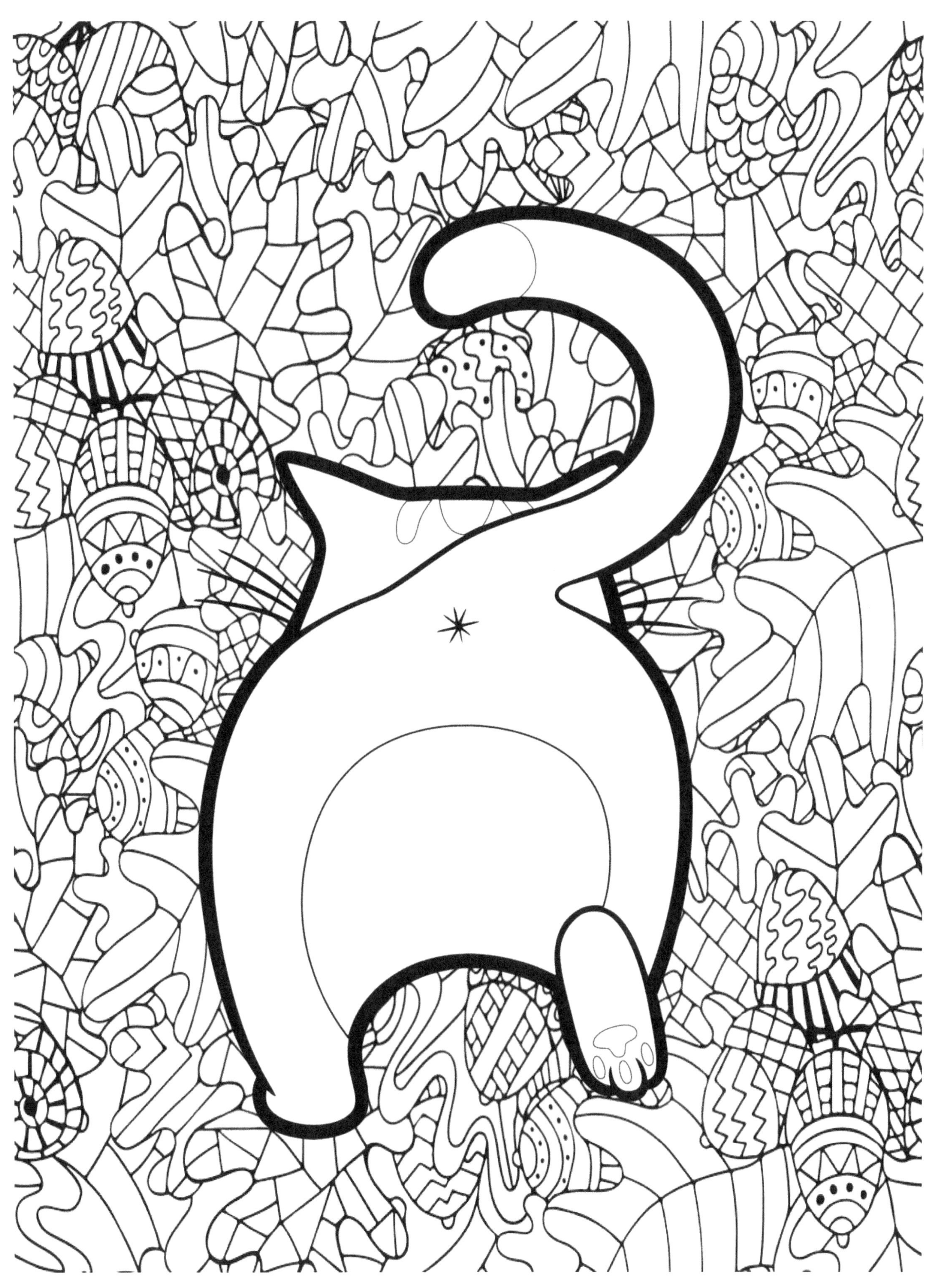

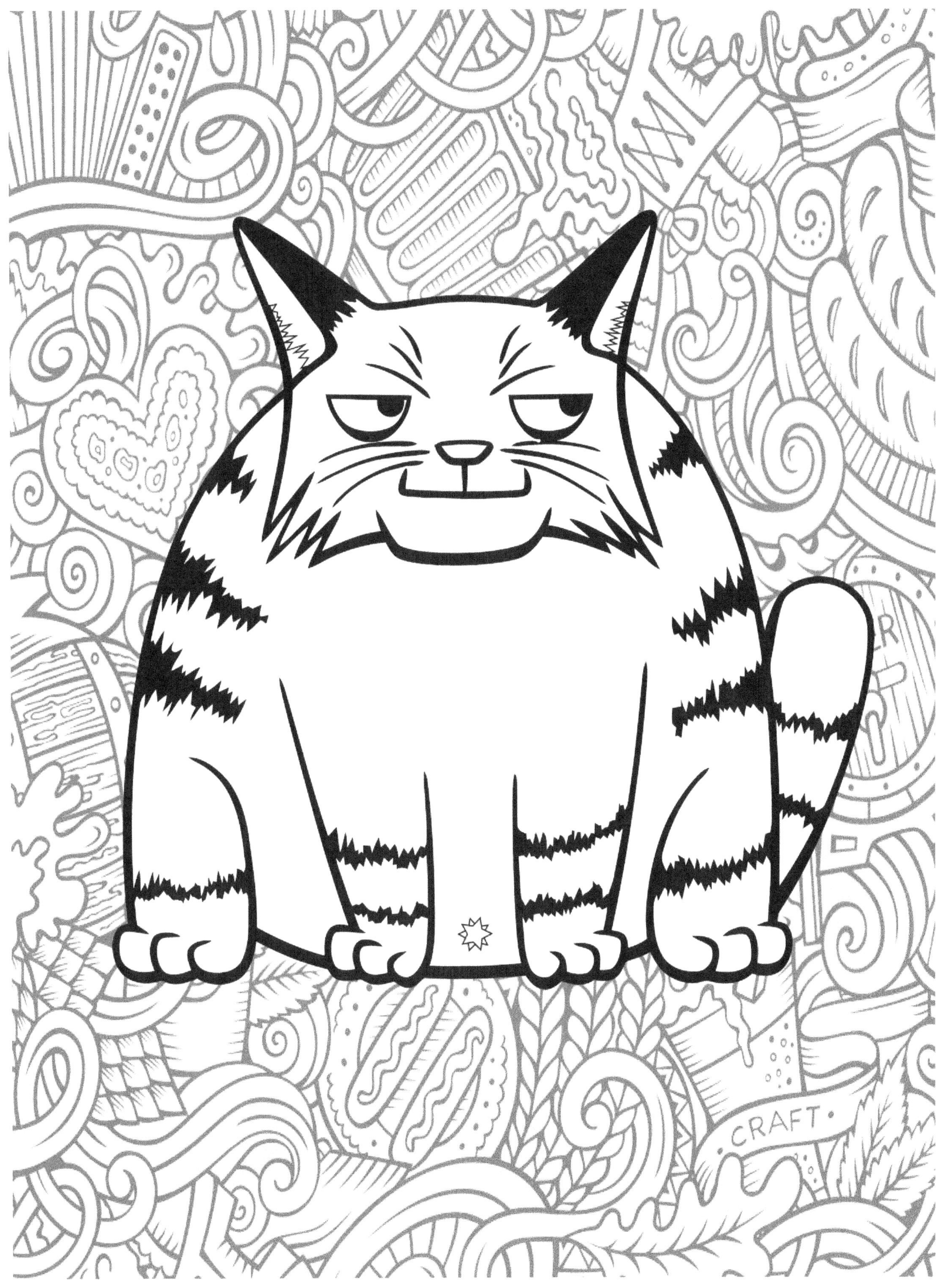
CRAFT

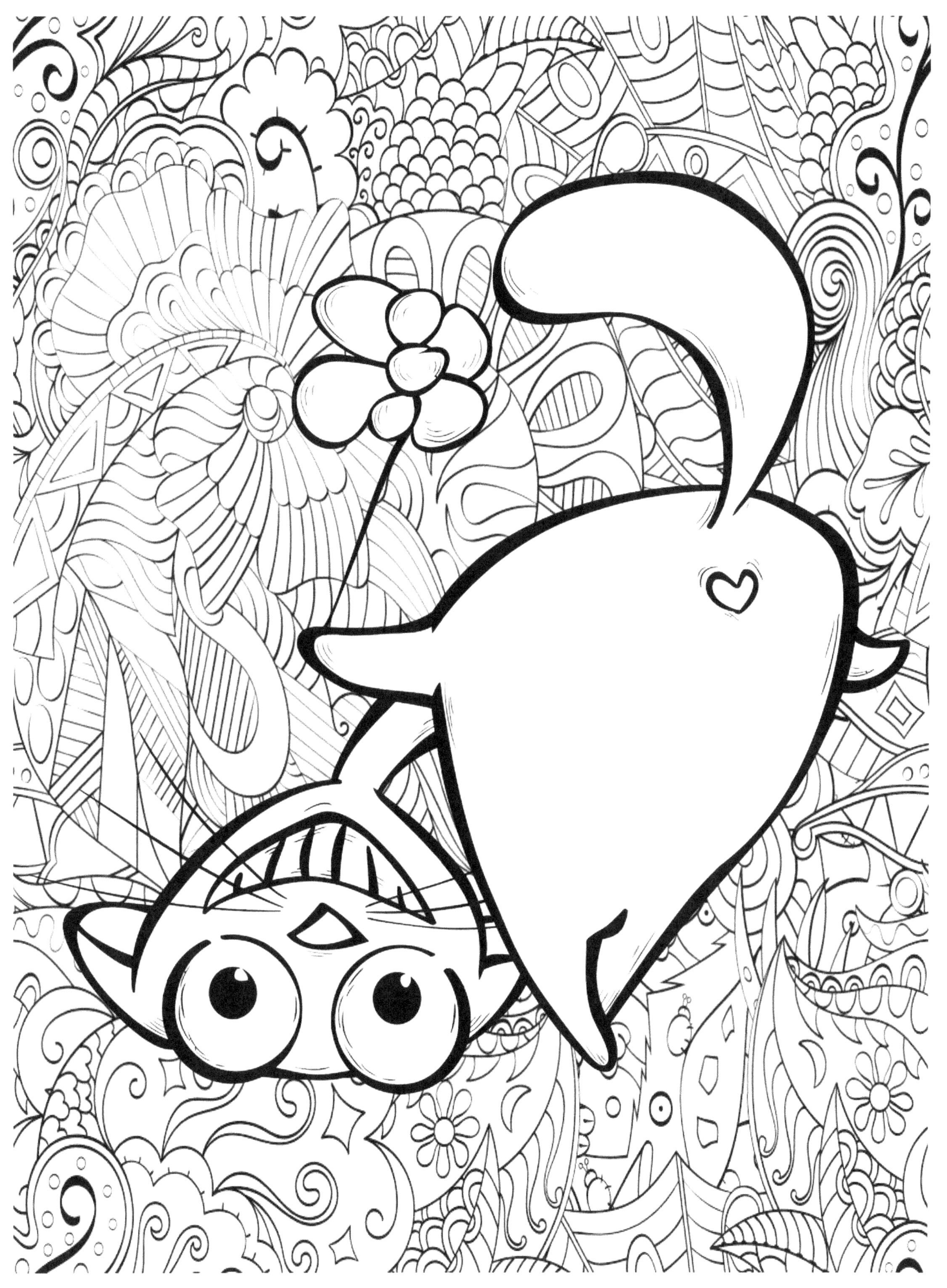

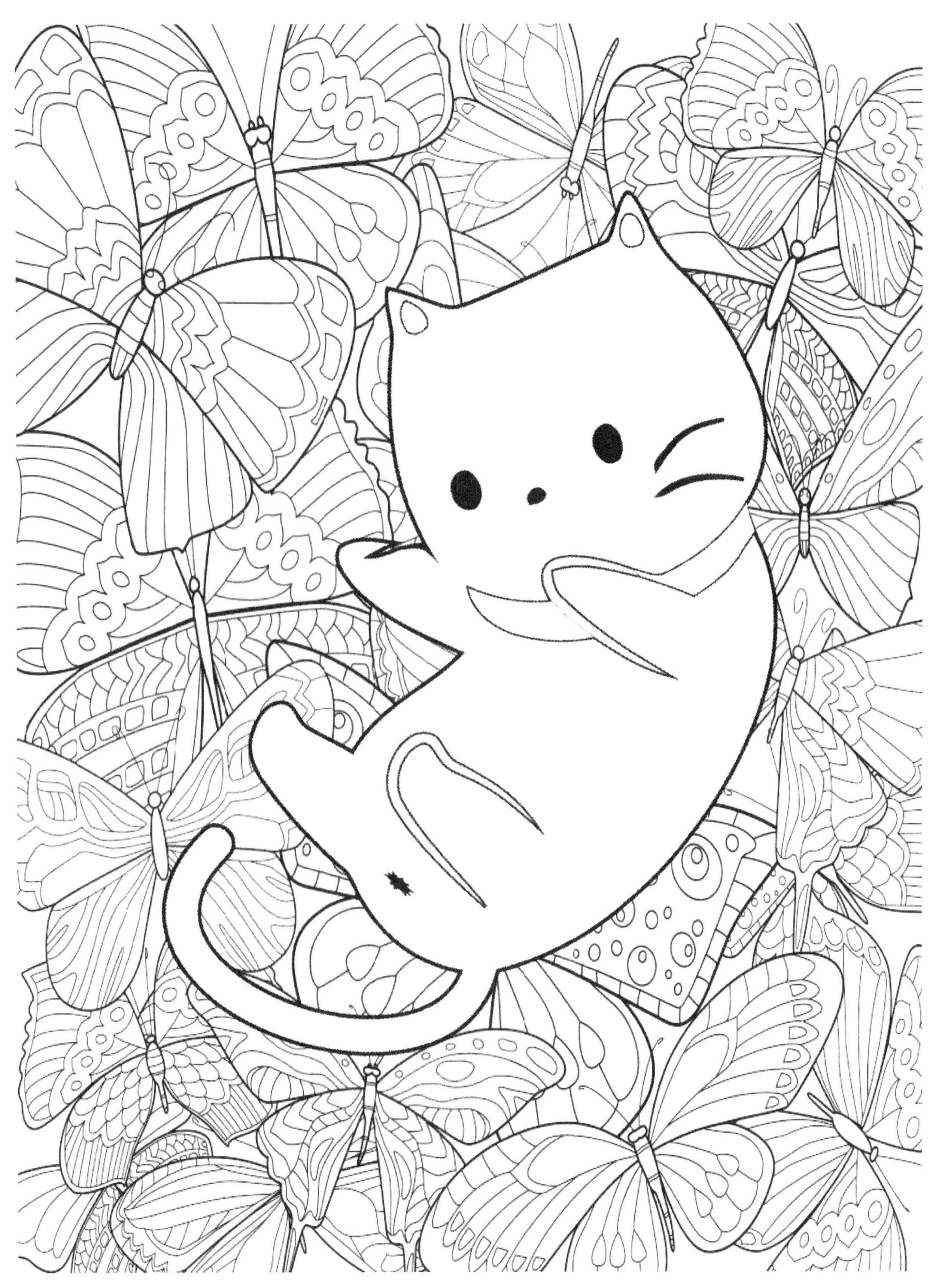

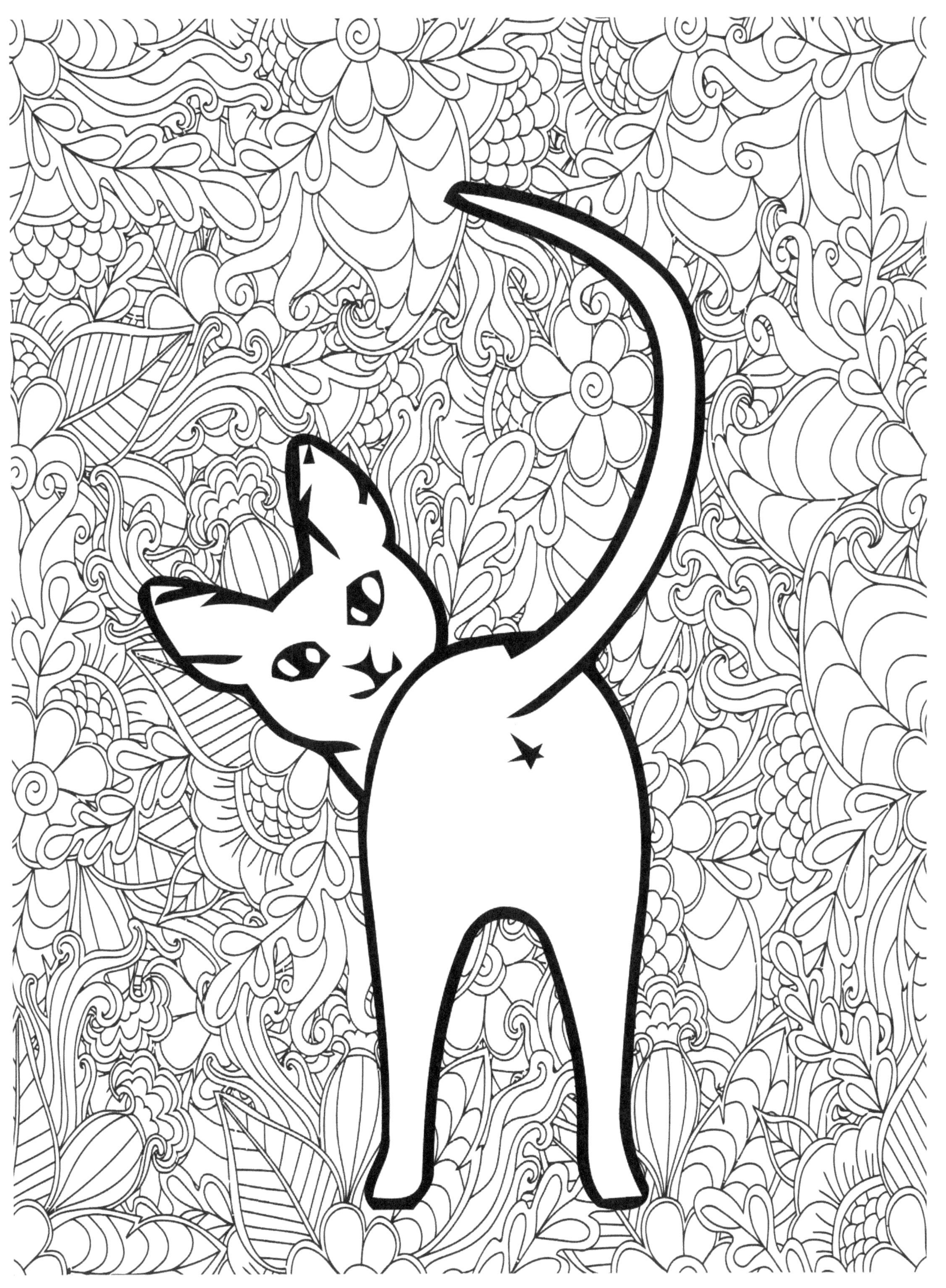

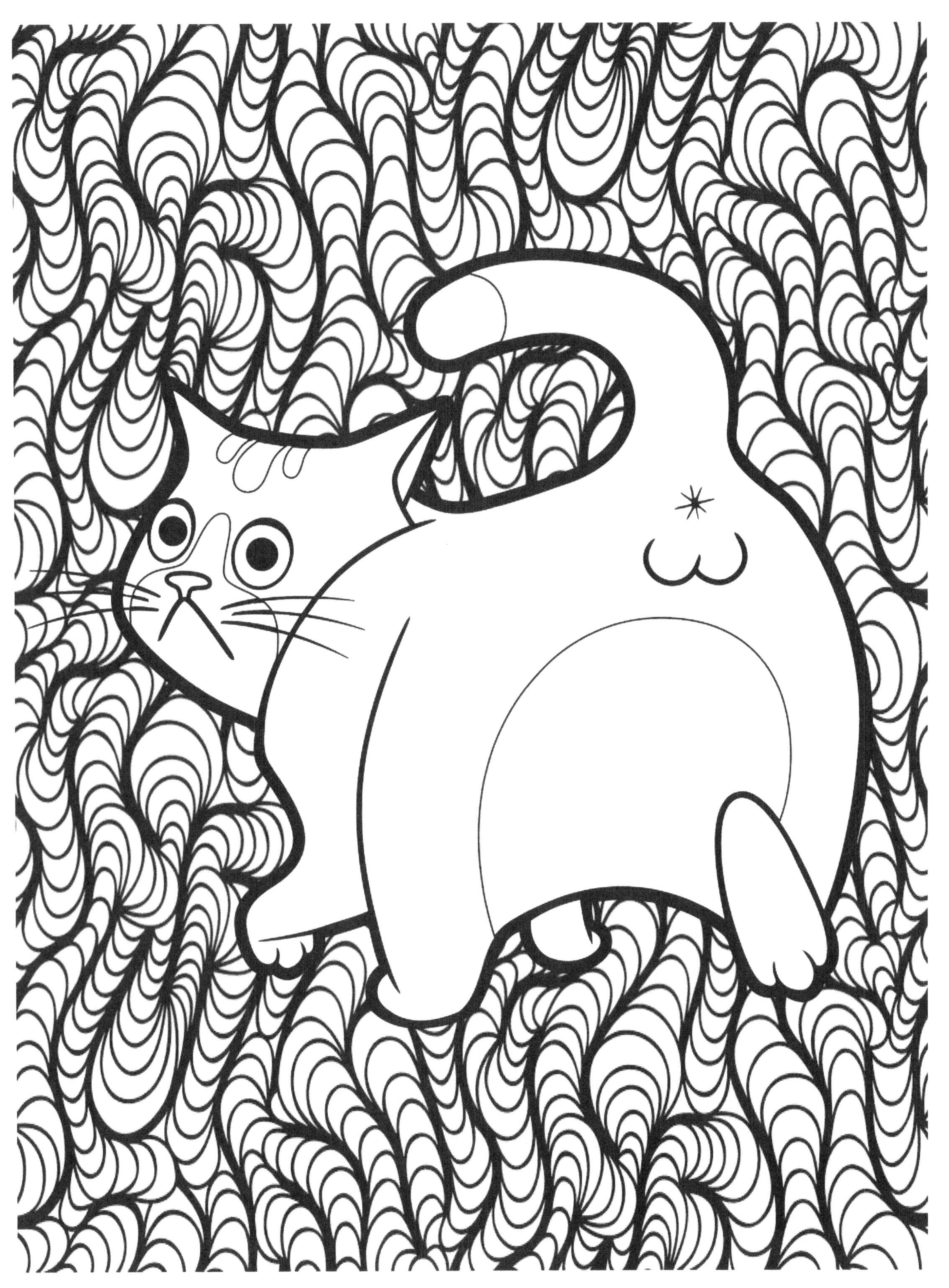

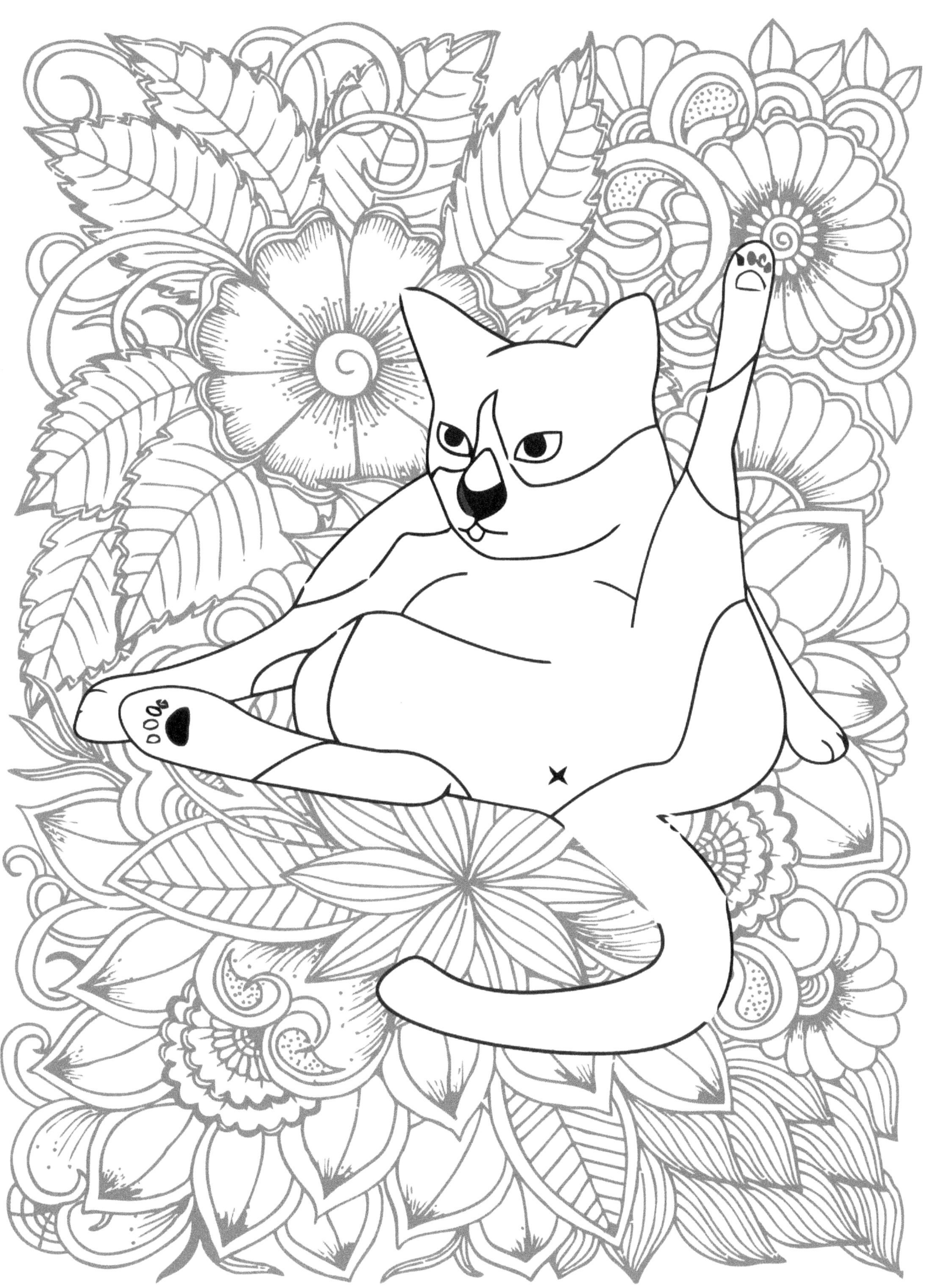

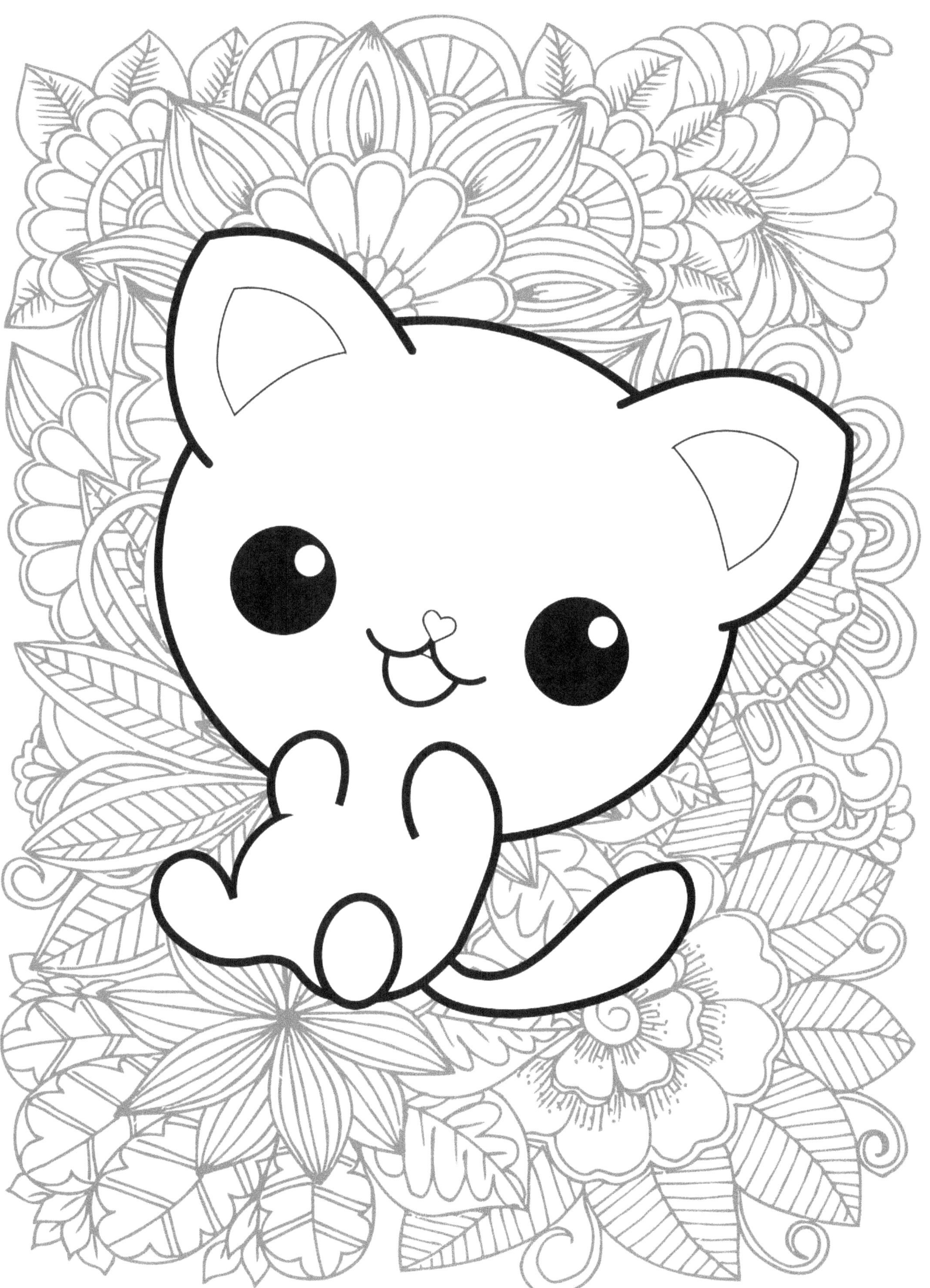

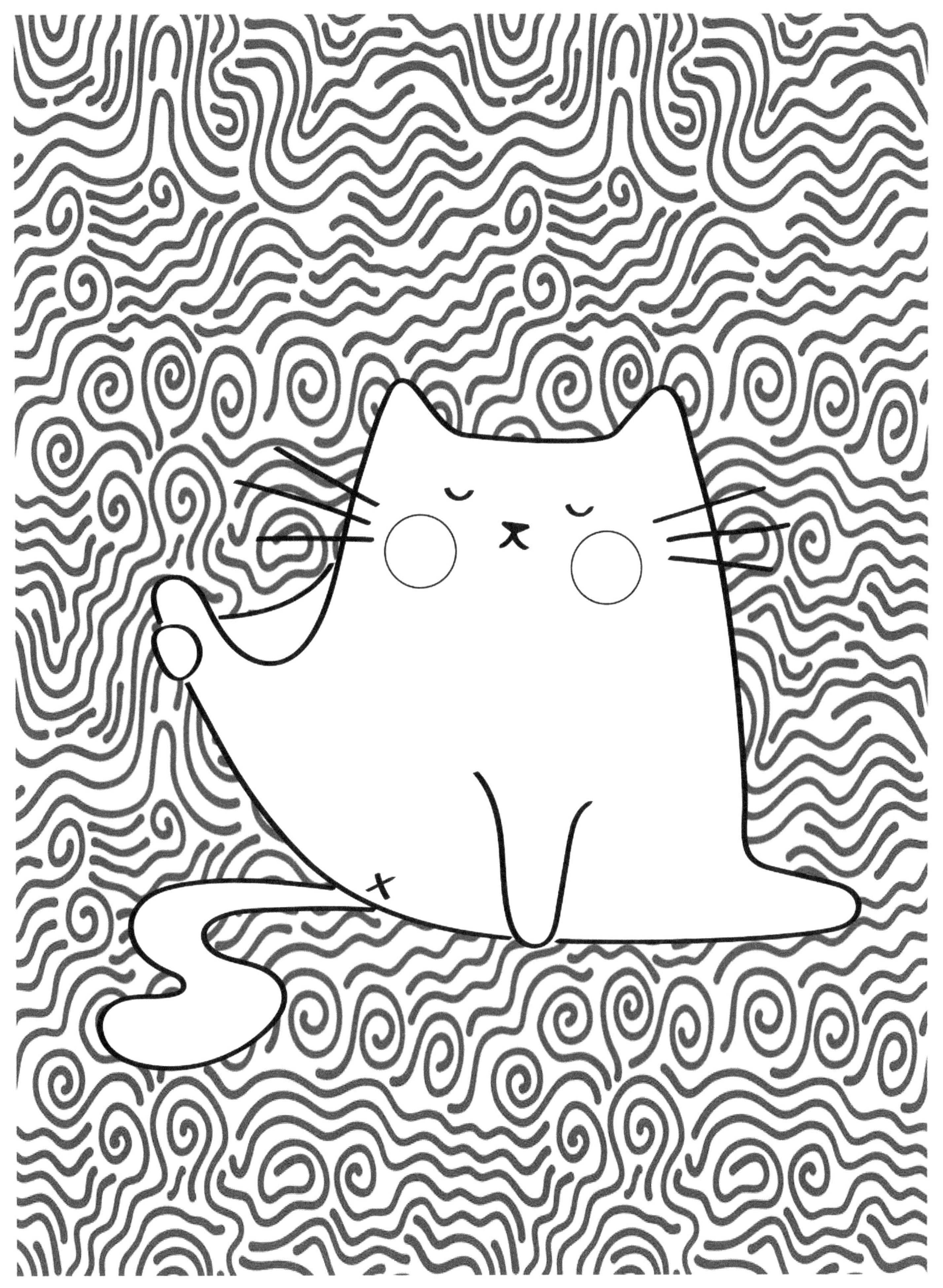

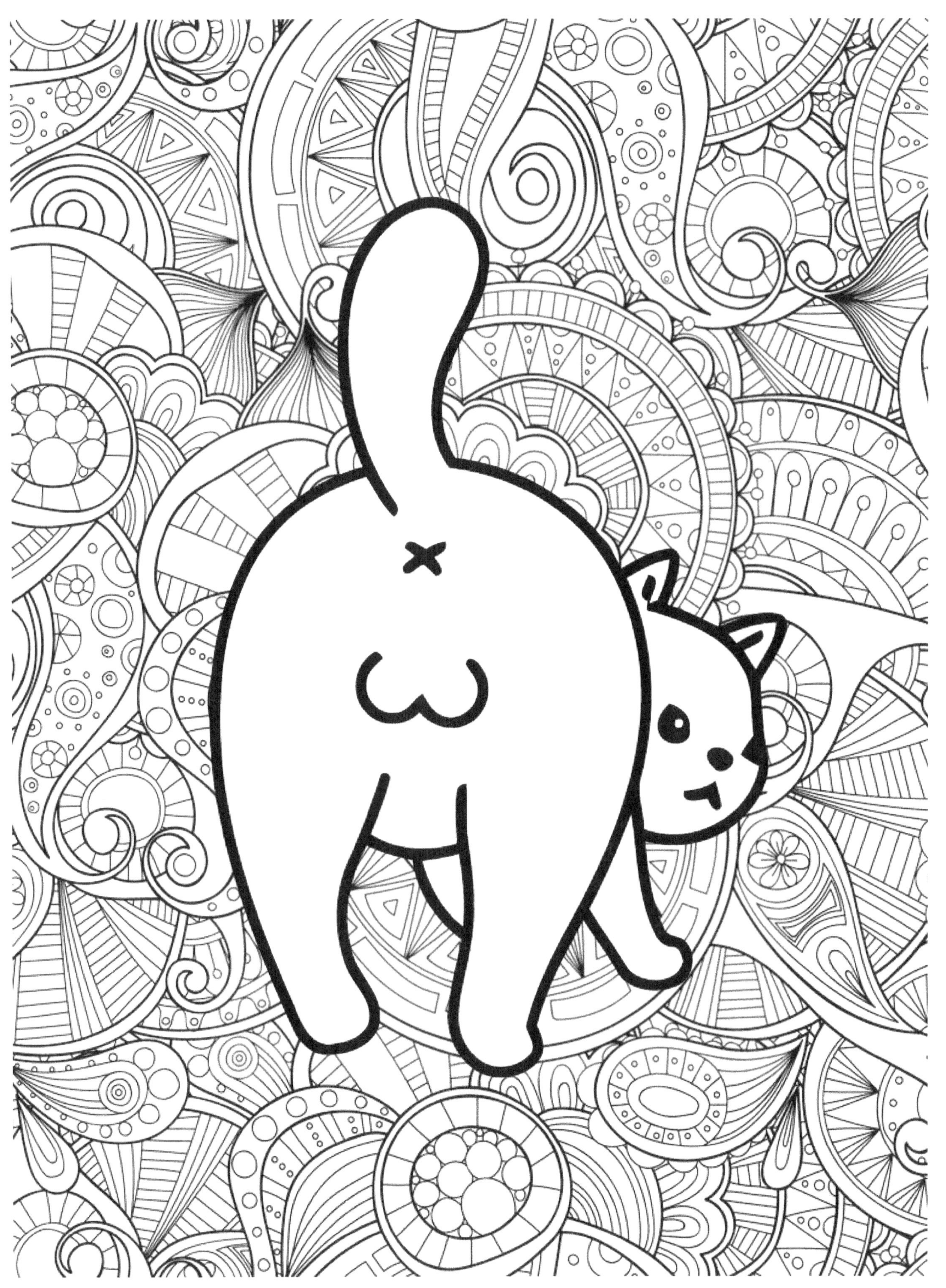

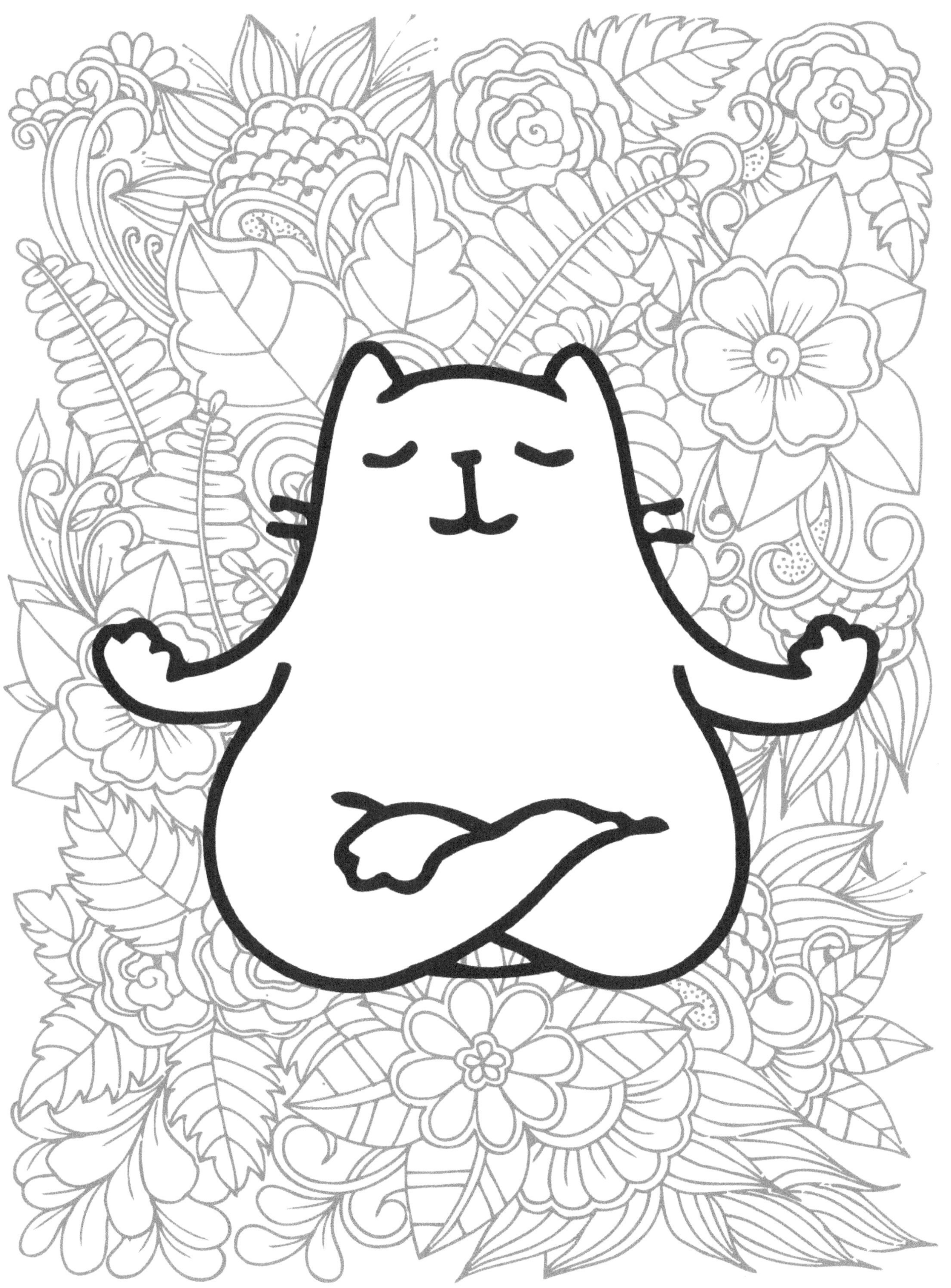

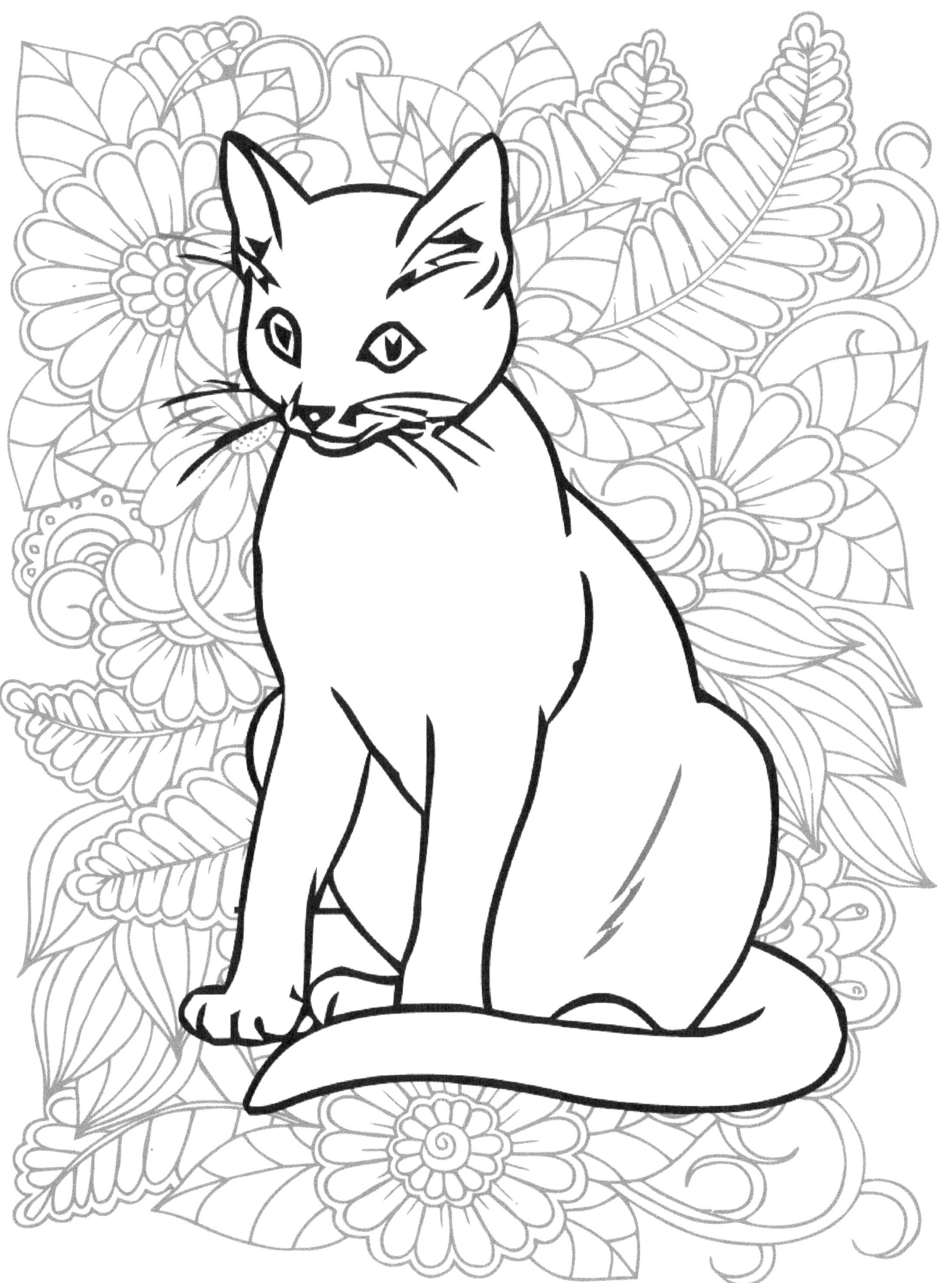

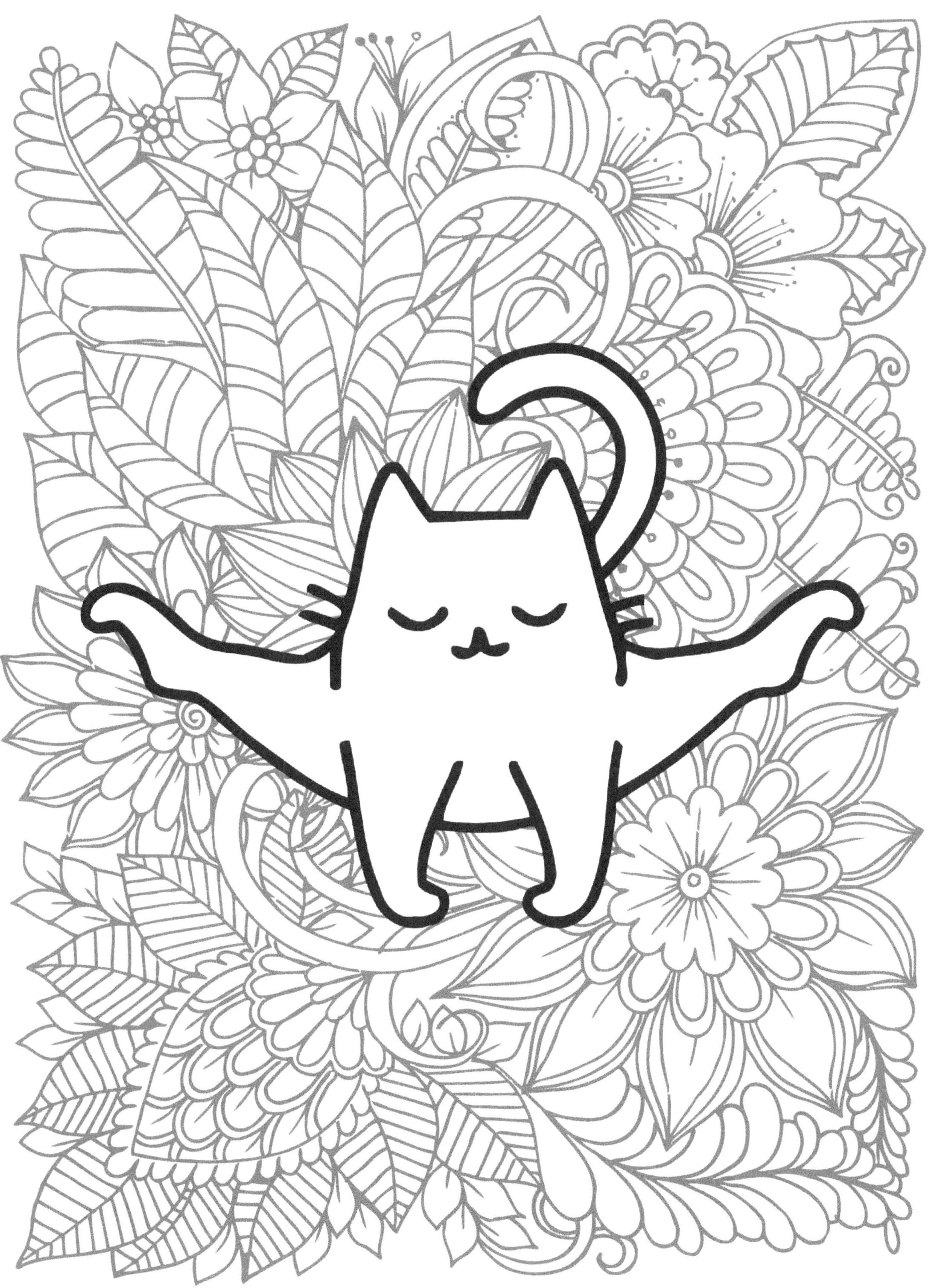

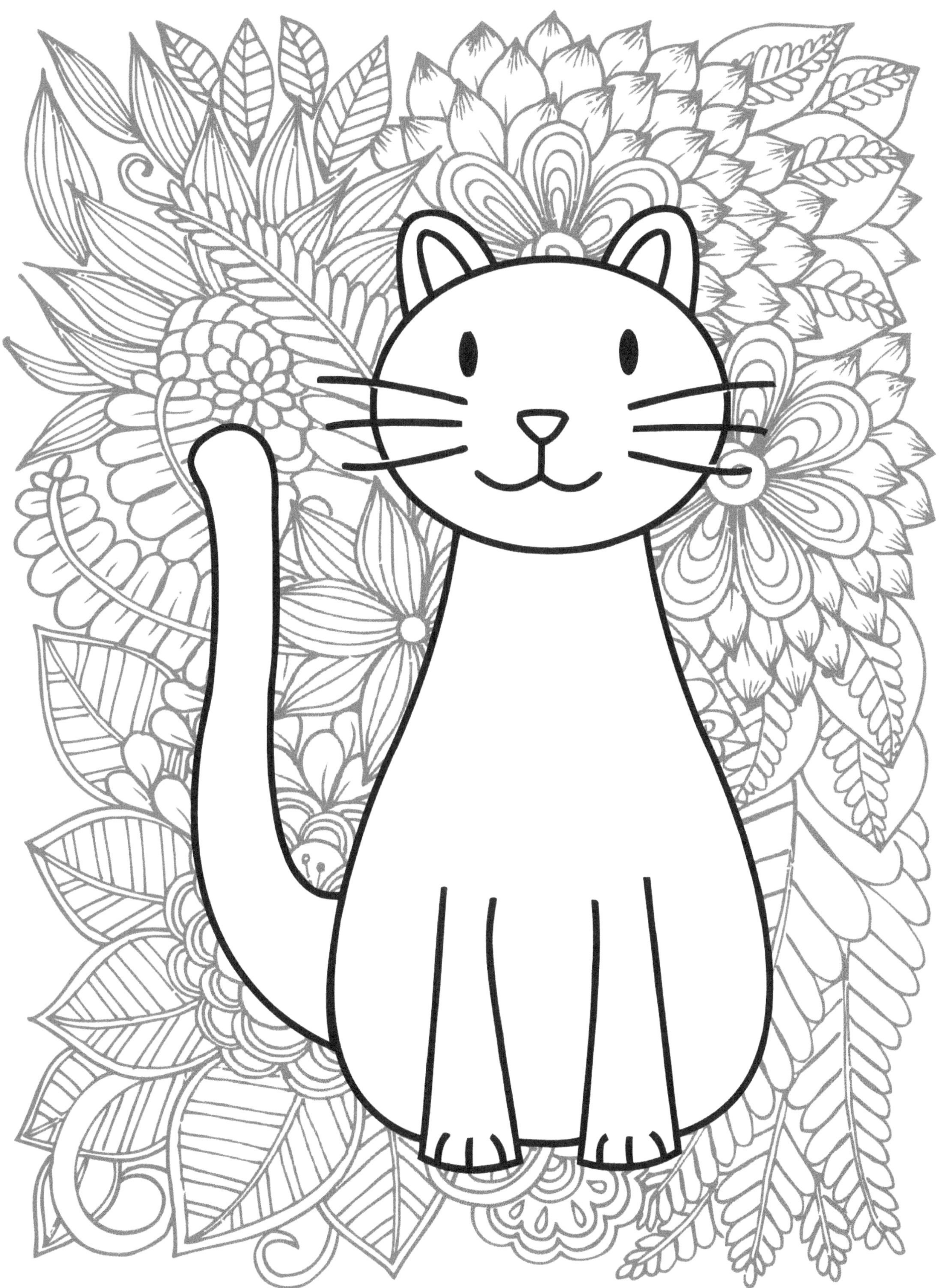

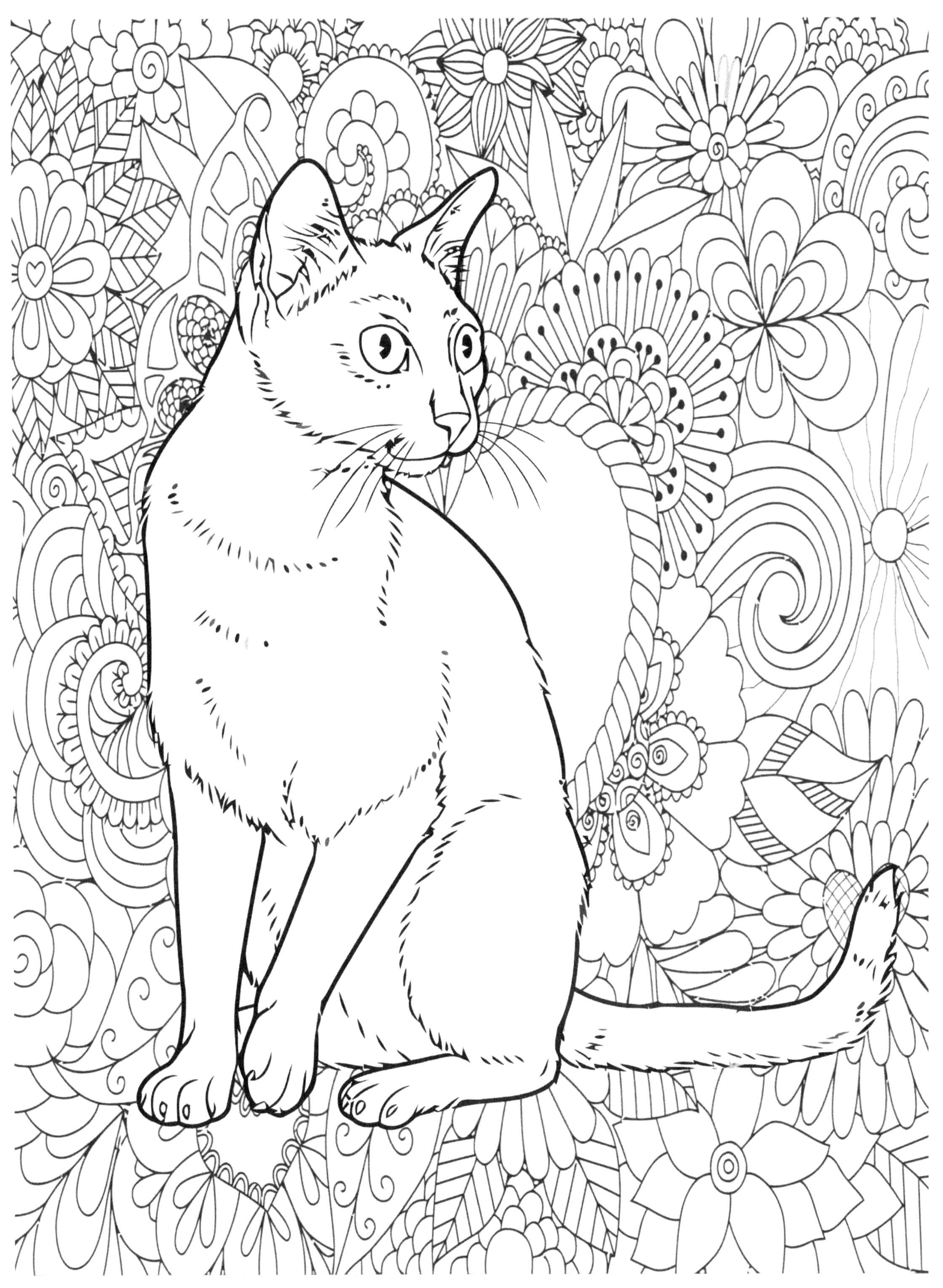

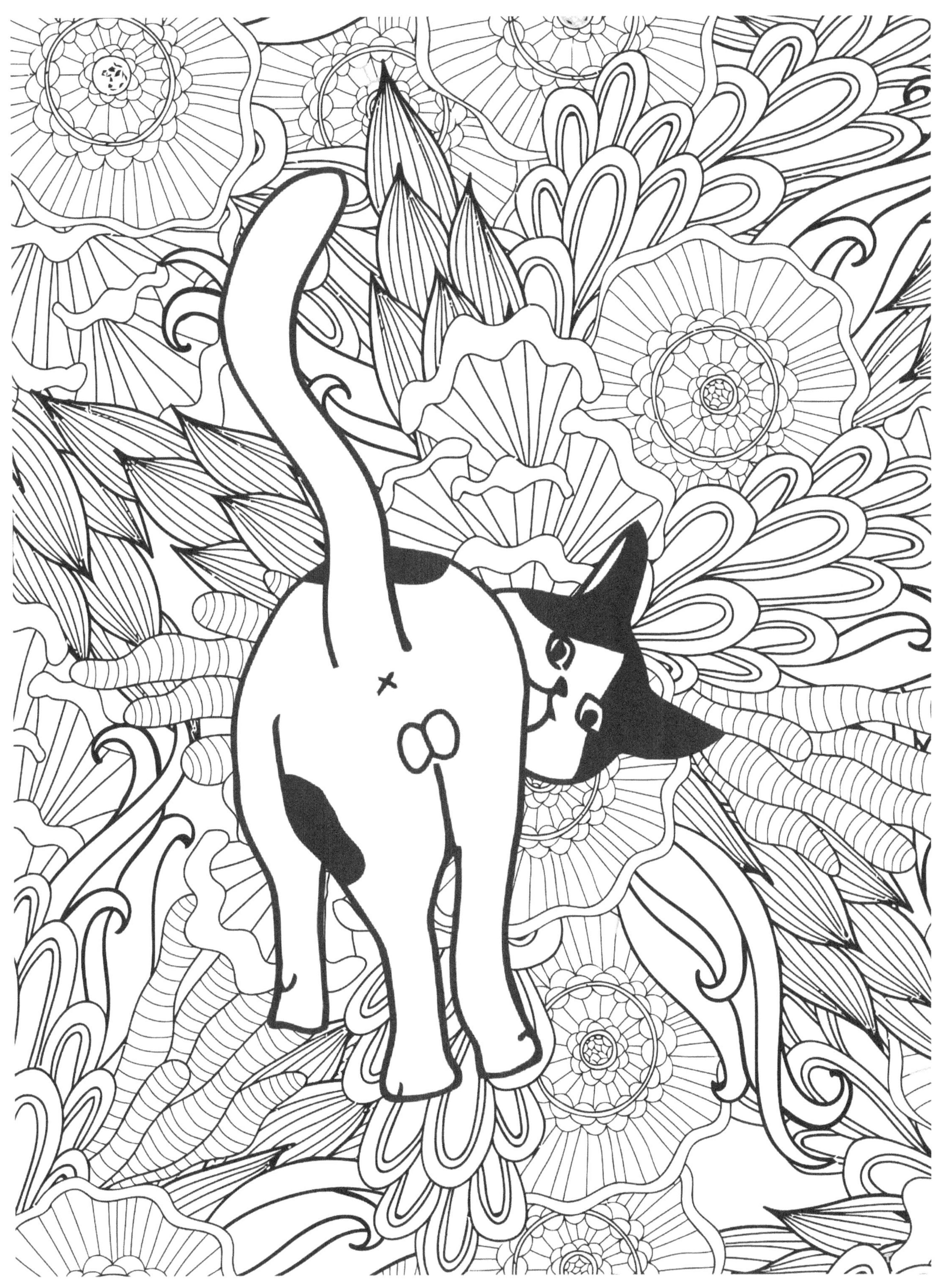

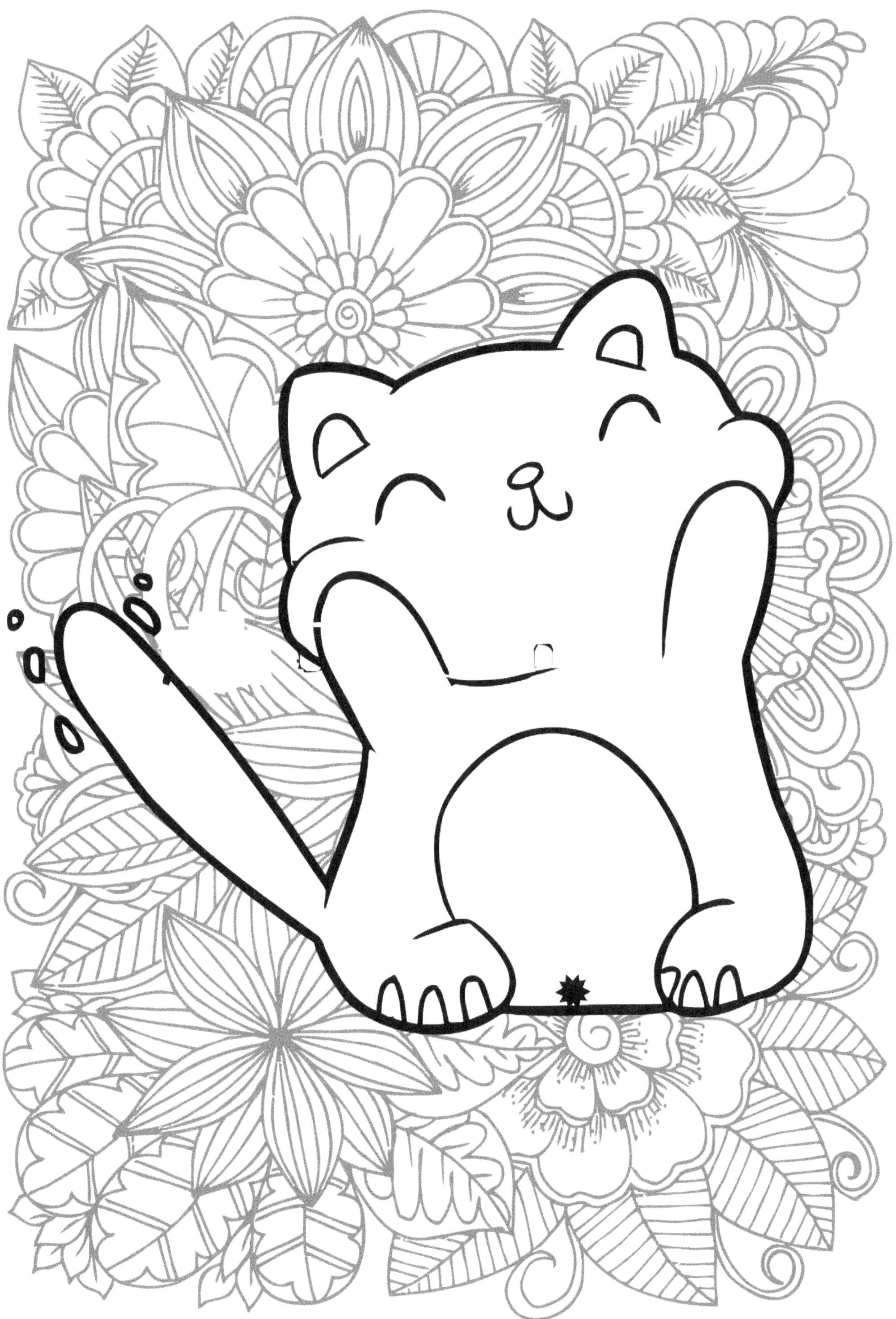

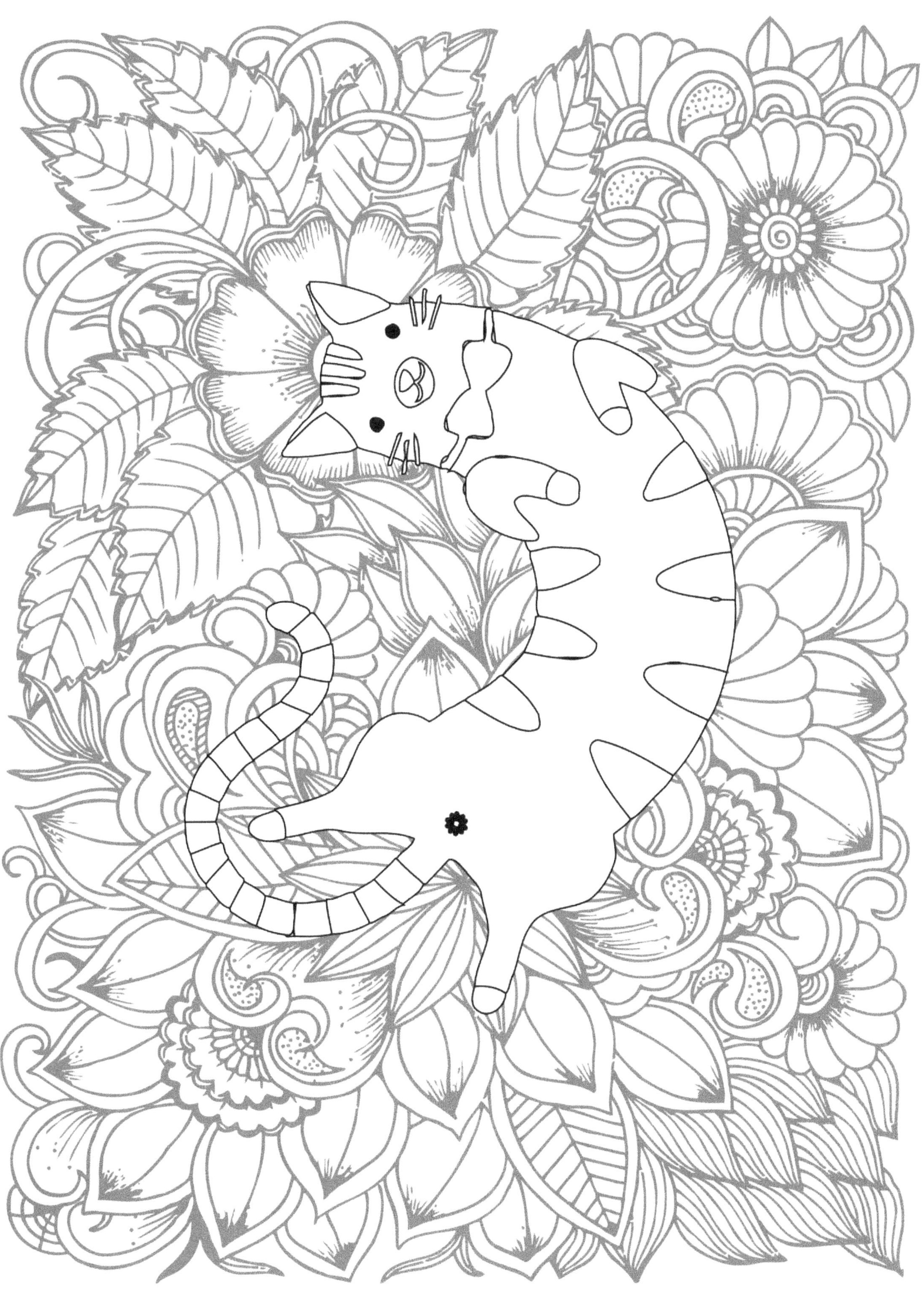